THE INDEPENDENT GUIDE TO WALT DISNEY AND UNIVERSAL ORLANDO 2020

G. COSTA

Limit of Liability and Disclaimer of Warranty:
The publisher has used its best efforts in preparing this book, and the information provided herein is provided "as is." Independent Guides and the author make no representation or warranties concerning the accuracy or completeness of the contents of this book and expressly disclaim any implied warranties of merchantability or fitness for any particular purpose and shall in no event be liable for any loss of profit or any other damage, including but not limited to special, incidental, consequential, or other damages.

Please read all signs before entering attractions, as well as the terms and conditions of any companies used. Prices are approximate and do fluctuate.

Contents

An Important Message Regarding the 2020 Pandemic:

At the time we were updating this guide , most of the world was under quarantine due to the global pandemic. As the parks reopen, the companies are understandably cautious about how they will make park visits safe for everyone. In the short term, at least, your visits may be affected by enhanced crowd control and social distancing measures and the possible cancellation (or changes) to shows, attractions, dining experiences, transportation and meet-and-greets. Check the official websites at www.disneyworld.disney.com and www.universalorlando.com for any changes that may affect your vacation.

Universal Orlando Overview

In 1971, Orlando was put on the map as the theme park capital of the world with the opening of Walt Disney World. It was a giant version of the Disneyland Resort that had opened in 1955 in Anaheim, California.

In the late 1980s, Universal announced it too would get in on the thrill game by opening its own East Coast theme park, similar to the one it owned in Hollywood.

Disney saw this new theme park as a significant competitor and decided that it would also build a theme park based around movie studios. Incredibly, Disney opened its studios park *before* the grand opening of Universal Studios Florida one year later. Disney's park was a rushed project, and Universal Studios Florida blew away the competition when it opened in 1990.

In 1995, Universal Orlando expanded with a second

theme park, Universal's Islands of Adventure. Three on-site resort hotels and an entertainment and dining district, CityWalk, were also added.

The original Universal Studios Florida park was also expanded with new areas to create a multi-day destination rivaling Disney.

In 1999, Universal's Islands of Adventure opened to rave reviews. It featured innovative attractions such as *The Amazing Adventures of Spider-Man* and *The*

Incredible Hulk Coaster.

The Universal Orlando Resort has continued to innovate with rides and areas such as *The Simpsons Ride* and *The Wizarding World of Harry Potter*. Visitor figures have sky-rocketed and collectively, both theme parks now welcome 16 million guests each year.

2020 marks an exciting year for the resort as it begins to work on building its third theme park.

Getting to Universal Orlando from Orlando Airport

By Car - Address: 6000 Universal Blvd, Orlando, FL. Universal Orlando is accessible by car from Interstate 4 (I-4), where you follow Universal Blvd north to the parking area. Parking garages open 90 minutes before the parks. Self-parking is $25 per day, and prime parking is $40. One parking area serves both theme parks and the water park. After parking, go through security and walk to the parks via CityWalk. For Volcano Bay, board a shuttle from Parking Level 1. Parking is 10 minutes' walk from the theme parks.

Shuttles and Taxis - Mears and Super Shuttle are reliable shuttles, although others are available. Prices from the airport are $30 to $35 per person roundtrip, or about $20 one-way. A taxi with Mears is about $55-$70 with a tip each way. UberX is about $28 to $34.

Public Transportation - At the airport, board Lynx bus number 42 or 111. Ask for a transfer ticket - ride to the 'Florida Mall' stop (25 minutes). At Florida Mall, transfer to bus route 37 and ride this for 45 minutes to the stop called 'Universal Boulevard and Hollywood Way' at the resort parking area. The total journey is about 1h15-1h30m (with departures every 25 minutes). We recommend using Google Maps to guide you along.

Tickets
All about Tickets

Ticket Types:
• A Single Park ticket gives access to one park per day (either *Universal Studios Florida, Islands of Adventure* or *Volcano Bay*)
• Park-to-Park tickets allow you to enter multiple parks on the same day.

One-day tickets vary in price depending on the visit date. Multi-day tickets do not change in price - see universalticketcalendar.com.

Single Park tickets allow you to ride every attraction in one park (except the *Hogwarts Express* which needs a Park-to-Park ticket).

Child prices apply to children aged 3 to 9. Kids under 3 get free entry. Prices exclude tax.

Getting your Tickets:
Advanced Tickets can be picked up from 'Will Call'

kiosks, printed at home, or mailed for an extra cost.

Save with Advanced Tickets:
All multi-day tickets are $20 cheaper when purchased in advance online at universalorlando.com than at the theme parks.
You can also buy tickets at on-site hotels, on the phone, and the Universal Orlando app and save $20 compared to park prices.

---

1 Day:
Single Park (USF or IOA): Adult - $115 to $135 and Child - $110 to $130
Park to Park (USF & IOA): Adult - $170 to $190 and Child - $165 to $185

---

2 Days:
One Park Per Day (USF or IOA):
Adult - $224.99
Child - $214.99

Park to Park (USF & IOA):
Adult - $284.99
Child - $274.99

Park to Park (USF & IOA & VB):
Adult - $339.99
Child - $329.99

USF - Universal Studios Florida, **IOA** - Islands of Adventure, **VB** - Volcano Bay

3 Days:
One Park Per Day (USF or IOA):
Adult - $244.99
Child - $234.99

One Park Per Day (USF or IOA or VB):
Adult - $299.99
Child - $289.99

Park to Park (USF & IOA):
Adult - $304.99
Child - $294.99

Park to Park (USF & IOA & VB):
Adult - $359.99
Child - $349.99

---

4 Days:
One Park Per Day (USF or IOA):
Adult - $254.99
Child - $244.99

One Park Per Day (USF or IOA or VB):
Adult - $319.99
Child - $309.99

Park to Park (USF & IOA):
Adult - $319.99
Child - $309.99

Park to Park (USF & IOA & VB):
Adult - $384.99
Child - $374.99

5 Days:
One Park Per Day (USF or IOA):
Adult - $264.99
Child - $254.99

One Park Per Day (USF or IOA or VB):
Adult - $339.99
Child - $329.99

Park to Park (USF & IOA):
Adult - $334.99
Child - $324.99

Park to Park (USF & IOA & VB):
Adult - $409.99
Child - $399.99

Hotels

Deciding where to stay while on vacation can be tricky: you have to consider price, availability, size, location, and amenities to find the perfect accommodation. Luckily, central Florida is renowned for having an incredible range of options to suit all tastes and budgets.

There are numerous hotels not located on Universal Orlando property that are cheaper than the on-site options. However, for the full Universal Orlando experience, we recommend staying at one of the on-site hotels. You will be just minutes away from the action, and the benefits of staying on-site are worth the cost, in our opinion.

There are four tiers of on-site hotels:
• Value – Endless Summer Resort
• Prime Value – Cabana Bay Beach Resort, and Aventura Hotel
• Preferred – Sapphire Falls Resort
• Premier – Portofino Bay Hotel, Hard Rock Hotel, and Royal Pacific Resort

Benefits available to on-site hotel guests:
• Early entry to *The Wizarding World of Harry Potter* 1 hour before the park opens to regular guests and early entry to Volcano Bay.
• Complimentary water taxis, shuttle buses, and walking paths to both theme parks and Universal CityWalk.
• Complimentary delivery of merchandise purchased throughout the resort to your hotel.
• Resort-wide charging privileges. Swipe your credit card at check-in and use your room key to charge purchases to your room. At check-out, you settle the balance as one amount.
• Complimentary Super Star Shuttle scheduled transportation to SeaWorld and Aquatica. This runs once a day from your hotel, and once or twice a day back to your hotel. Seats are reserved at the concierge desk.
• Optional wake-up call from a Universal character.
• Use of the Golf Universal Orlando program.

Guests at Royal Pacific Resort, Portofino Bay Hotel, and Hard Rock Hotel also enjoy these added benefits:
• FREE Universal Express Pass - Unlimited ride access to skip the regular lines at both theme parks all day.
• Priority seating at select restaurants throughout both theme parks and CityWalk.

All room prices in this section are nightly rates and include tax - they are based on a 3-night stay for 2 adults; food prices listed in this guide do not include tax.

Fitness and Pools

Fitness Suites:
All on-site hotels have complimentary fitness suites for their guests.

Although not widely advertised, guests staying at most on-site hotels* can use any of the fitness suites.

This means that a guest from Cabana Bay Beach Resort could, for example, visit the gym at the Hard Rock Hotel with their room key.

*Guests staying at Endless Summer Resort cannot use other hotel's gyms.

Pools:
All the on-site hotels have impressive pools and you can 'pool hop'. If you are staying at most on-site resort hotels*, you can use the pool of any resort (and even settle the tab at another hotel with your hotel key). A fantastic benefit!

Who wouldn't want to try the fun pools at Cabana Bay, the magnificent one at the Hard Rock, and then finish the day with a dip at the Sapphire Falls pool?

*Guests staying at Endless Summer Resort cannot pool hop.

On-Site Amenities

Parking:
Parking is $27 per night at Hard Rock Hotel, Portofino Bay, and Royal Pacific Resort. It is $25 at Sapphire Falls, $17 at Cabana Bay and Aventura Hotel, and $14 at the Endless Summer resort. Hotel guests do not get a discount on this rate.

Day guests who park in the hotel lots pay based on the length of their stay, unless eating at the on-site restaurants when they can get up to 3 hours of complimentary parking.

Internet Access:
Standard in-room Wi-Fi access is free. For higher speed access, there is a premium option for a fee.

The lobby and pool areas at all the on-site hotels have free Wi-Fi, which you can access regardless of whether you are staying at the hotel or not.

Pet rooms:
Pet rooms are available at all Premier and Preferred hotels. A cleaning fee of $50 per night applies, up to $150 per room.

Refrigerators:
All rooms at all the on-site hotels include a mini-refrigerator for your use.

Character Dining:
The Royal Pacific Resort, Portofino Bay Hotel, and Hard Rock Hotel offer character-dining experiences where characters visit your table for you to meet, chat, and take photos, while you eat.

Characters vary from Scooby-Doo to Shrek and even The Minions. Character dining takes place once or twice a week between 6:30pm and 9:30pm. You can visit any resort's restaurant, even if you are not a hotel guest.

Kids Camps:
Kids camps are available at Royal Pacific Resort, Portofino Bay Hotel, and Hard Rock Hotel in the evenings. This keeps kids occupied with activities while parents spend quality time together.

Guests from any hotel can use the Kids Camps at other hotels. Prices are about $15 per child per hour.

Endless Summer Resort

With over 2000 rooms, this Value hotel is well-priced for budget-conscious guests.

Endless Summer Resort is made up of two hotels - Surfside Inn & Suites and Dockside Inn & Suites. The two hotels are not connected but guests can use facilities at both hotels.

This resort is *not* connected to the main Universal area with the two theme parks, and CityWalk. To travel between here and the main Universal Orlando area means either walking approx. 1 mile or using the free shuttle bus.

Standard rooms are comparable with Aventura

Hotel, but the suites at this hotel are smaller than those at the other hotels.

There is no Table Service restaurant at this resort.

Transport: Shuttle buses (5 to 10 mins travel time).
Room Size and Prices:
Standard rooms are 313 ft² ($117-240), and 2-bedroom suites are 440 ft² ($172-314).
Activities: Arcade room; fitness center; pool; a store; poolside bar.
Dining: Each hotel has a bar, food court, Starbucks and pizza delivery.

Aventura Hotel

This 600-room Prime Value hotel is one step up from Endless Summer Resort.

This hotel is the most technologically advanced place to stay at Universal.

The food hall features many different cuisines, but there is no Table Service restaurant. There are three bars including one on the roof offering amazing views, as well as a Starbucks.

This hotel is next door to Volcano Bay water park, so you can simply walk over to the water park in minutes.

Transport: Walking paths (20 to 25 mins) & shuttle buses.
Room Size and Prices: Standard rooms are 314 ft^2 ($161-302) and kids suites are 591 ft^2 ($288-556).
Activities: Arcade room; fitness center; pool and splash zone; a store; rooftop and poolside bars.

Dining: Poolside bar, lobby side, rooftop bar, and food court.

Cabana Bay Beach Resort

This 2200-room, Retro-1950s and 1960s Prime Value hotel is a middle-ground for the location and amenities versus the price.

The 10-lane bowling alley is unheard of at any other hotel (extra charge).

The main pool is 10,000 ft^2 with a water slide, and the smaller 8000 ft^2 pool has a sandy beach. There is also a 700ft-long lazy river.

The hotel has direct walking access to Volcano Bay water park in just minutes.

Large families and groups have the option of 2-bedroom suites for up 6 guests. Standard rooms sleep up to 4 guests.

Transport: Walking paths (20 to 25 mins) & shuttle buses.
Room Size and Prices: Standard rooms are 300 ft^2 ($161-301), family suites are 430 ft^2 (£212-392)and 2-bedroom suites are 772 ft^2 ($449-$702).
Activities: Bowling alley; arcade room; two pools – one with a waterslide; s'mores fire pit; hot hub; poolside movies and

activities; a store; and a fitness center.
Dining: Poolside bar, food court, Table Service restaurant, lounge bar, Starbucks, poolside bar and grill, in-room pizza delivery.

Loews Sapphire Falls Resort

This 1000-room, 83-suite resort is a Preferred category hotel. It features a Caribbean-inspired design.

This beautiful, tropical destination is a step up from Cabana Bay in amenities and theming. The centerpiece is a 16,000ft^2 pool - the largest in Orlando - with two sandy beaches, cabanas, and a water slide.

This hotel does not include Express Pass access, nor priority seating at restaurants.

On Fridays, there is a paid buffet and a show called Caribbean Carnival.

Transport: Water taxis, pedicabs, walking paths (15 to 20 mins) & shuttle buses.
Room Size and Prices:

Standard rooms are 364 ft^2 ($227-381), and suites start at 529 ft^2 ($328-764).
Activities: Pool, two beaches, a hot tub, water jet play jet and a waterslide; fire pit for s'mores; fitness center with a dry sauna; arcade room; and a store.
Dining: Table Service restaurant, poolside bar and tapas-style menu, rum and ceviche bar, and food court.

Loews Royal Pacific Resort

This 1000-room, Preferred category hotel is themed to a tropical paradise.

A world away from the hustle and bustle of the theme parks, yet, they are conveniently right next door. There is a large pool with movies and cabanas, a gym, steam and sauna facilities, and a whirlpool, plus an on-site coin laundry.

Enjoy the free Torch Lighting Ceremony with hula dancers and fire jugglers.

The hotel hosts the Despicable Me Character Breakfast on Saturdays ($40 per adult & $25 per child).

The hotel's laid back Polynesian vibe and its location make it a solid choice - this hotel includes unlimited complimentary Express Pass access.

Transport: Water taxis, pedicabs, walking paths (15 to 20 mins) & shuttle buses. **Room Size and Prices**: Standard rooms are 375 ft^2 ($289-584), and suites start at 650 ft^2 ($578-753).

Activities: A large pool, volleyball court, water play area, gym, croquet, poolside activities, a torch-lighting ceremony, and Wantilan Luau dinner show. **Dining**: Poolside bar & grill, Table Service restaurant, bar, lounge & sushi bar, and Hawaiian dinner show.

Hard Rock Hotel Orlando

This rock 'n' roll, Premier tier hotel has 650 rooms, including 33 suites. It is the closest hotel to the parks.

Feel like rock 'n' roll royalty at this hotel - lively, yet laid back. The highlight is the 12,000ft^2, white sand pool with an underwater sound system! There are poolside 'dive-in movies,' and dive-in concerts.

DJ lessons are held in the lobby in peak season, and you can even rent out a

Fender by AXE guitar at no extra cost during your stay.

This hotel is the closest to CityWalk and the theme parks, and is right next door to Universal Studios Florida; this makes a midday dip in the pool a real possibility.

Transport: Water taxis, pedicabs, walking paths (5 mins to USF and 10 mins to IOA) and shuttle buses. **Room Size and Prices**: 375 ft^2 for a standard room ($332-651)

Activities: Pool, Jacuzzis, volleyball court, and a gym. arcade room; and a store. **Dining**: Bar and Quick Service, ice cream and pizza place, Table service dining, buffet breakfast, and a bar.

Loews Portofino Bay Hotel

Portofino Bay is a 750-room Premier level luxury resort themed to the seaside Italian village of Portofino.

The hotel has three pools - one with a waterslide, the other has a jacuzzi, and the quiet pool overlooks the bay. In peak season, there is a 'Dive-In Movie.' Pool cabanas are available to rent.

The Mandara Spa offers a variety of experiences including massages, facials, nail services, waxing, and haircuts.

In the evenings, weather permitting, the hotel has live music and classical singers, and guests can enjoy the atmosphere.

Transport: Water taxis, pedicabs, walking paths (20

mins) & shuttle buses. **Room Size and Prices**: 450 ft^2 for a standard room ($404-$668), and kids' suites are $697 to $1158. **Activities**: 3 pools, poolside movies, spa, live music. **Dining**: Upscale bar, gourmet Table service restaurant, coffee shop, Quick Service restaurant, bar with snacks, bar and grill, buffet and Table Service restaurant.

Universal Studios Florida

Universal Studios Florida opened in 1990 as the Floridian cousin to the popular Universal Studios theme park in Hollywood. The original idea of the park was to experience how movies were made.

Universal allows you to ride and experience the movies instead of just seeing how they are made. The park hosted 10.7 million guests in 2018.

Note: Average attraction waits noted in this section are estimates for busy summer days during school breaks. Wait times may well be lower at other times of the year. They may also occasionally be higher, especially during the week of 4th July, Thanksgiving, Christmas, New Year and other public holidays.

Where we list food prices, this information was accurate during our last visit to the restaurant. We include a sample of the food on offer and not the full menu. Meal prices listed do not include a drink or sales tax, unless otherwise stated. When an attraction is listed as requiring lockers, all loose items must be stored in complimentary locker storage outside the attraction.

Attraction Key

 Does it have Express Pass?

 Is there an On-Ride Photo?

 Average wait times (on peak days)

 Do I need to place my belongings in a locker before riding?

 Minimum height (in inches)

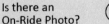 Ride/Show Length

What is Express Pass?
It's an optional front-of-the-line service which is included in some Universal hotels' room rates or can be purchased individually.

You can read more about it on page 34.

Production Central

Production Central is home to **Guest Services** where you can request disability passes, make dining reservations, ask questions, and give feedback.

You will find **lockers, stroller and wheelchair rentals, Lost and Found**, and **First Aid**.

You will also find the **American Express Passholder Lounge**, opposite the Shrek shop. This lounge is reserved for guests who use an AmEx card to buy park tickets or an annual pass directly from Universal.

Inside the AmEx lounge, you will find bottled water, snacks, and phone charging facilities. Simply show your ticket receipt, the ticket itself, and your AmEx card for entry. Guests must use an AmEx card to purchase their theme park tickets (either on UniversalOrlando.com or at the park ticket windows) to have access to this lounge.

If you need to mail something, you can drop off your **letters and postcards** at the mailbox, located to the left as you come in after the turnstiles, to the right of the lockers.

Stamps can be purchased from the On Location shop here on the Front Lot.

Family & Health Services, which includes a nursing room, is here too.

Hollywood Rip Ride Rockit

Hollywood Rip Ride Rockit is a unique roller coaster that dominates the skyline.

On this ride, you get to choose from several songs to play during your ride. Music pumps into your ears through in-seat speakers as your adrenaline races. Straight after the first drop, you enter a unique 'loop' but stay upright all the way around - a really unique experience.

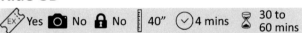
Yes 📷 Yes 🔒 Yes | 51-79" | ⌄ 2 mins | ⧖ 45 to 90 mins

As well as on-ride photos, you can buy a music video of your ride using on-board cameras! A Single Rider line is available at this attraction.

TRANSFORMERS: The Ride-3D

TRANSFORMERS is a 3D screen-based moving dark ride. The storyline follows the Autobots protecting the AllSpark from the Decepticons.

Your ride vehicle moves from set to set, acting as a moving simulator immersing

Yes 📷 No 🔒 No | 40" | ⌄ 4 mins | ⧖ 30 to 60 mins

you in the action.

TRANSFORMERS: The Ride is doubly impressive to fans of the movie franchise, but it can be enjoyed by everyone.

A Single Rider line is available - it usually reduces your wait to about half of the regular wait. Children between 40" and 48" must be accompanied by a supervising companion.

Shrek 4-D

Stepping into Shrek 4D, you know you are getting into a different kind of attraction. The unique part of this attraction is the seats, which act like personal

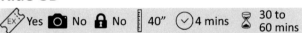
Yes 📷 No 🔒 No | N/A | ⌄ 12 mins | ⧖ 15 to 45 mins

simulators. Stationary seats are also available.

The movie is great fun with some corny jokes and lots of jabs at Disney thrown in.

Despicable Me: Minion Mayhem

A simulator ride featuring 4D effects and the characters from Despicable Me. A must-do for fans of the movies!

Due to the popularity of the characters, waits are almost always very long.

Yes 📷 No 🔒 No | 40" | ⌄ 4 mins | ⧖ 45 to 90 mins

Top Tip: A stationary version of this attraction operates with benches at the front of the theater. These do not move, but you see the 3D.

Children between 40" and 48" must be accompanied.

Children under 40" may ride in stationary seating.

Dining

Universal Studios' Classic Monster Cafe – Quick Service. Accepts Universal Dining Plan. Serves chicken, lasagne, cheeseburgers, pizza, and other fast-food. Entrées are $13 to $20.

New York

Revenge of The Mummy

Revenge of The Mummy is one of the most fun coasters in Orlando. It starts as a slow-moving dark ride and turns into a traditional roller coaster.

The ride tells its story well and immerses you in the atmosphere. It is a great thrill, with surprises throughout. The queue line is also incredibly detailed and contains several interactive elements.

 Yes Yes Yes 48" 4 mins 20 to 60 mins

A Single Rider queue line is available. We recommend first-timers see the regular standby line before using Single Rider.

The Blues Brothers Show

See Jake and Elwood, the Blues Brothers, take to the stage in this show. Unlike other shows where you sit in a show-style amphitheater, *The Blues Brothers Show* takes place on a small stage in the street with a street-performer feel to it.

Crowds are not very big, and most people walk in and out during the show - it is worth stopping by.

Rock Climbing

Next to *Revenge of the Mummy*, there is a small alleyway that has a 50-foot tall rock-climbing wall. Climb it and once you reach the top, ring the bell to claim victory!

Race Through New York Starring Jimmy Fallon

This is a 3D simulated adventure with American comedian Jimmy Fallon.

Yes No No 40" 25 mins None

Inside NBC's Studios, instead of a standard queue line, you explore two rooms with NBC and Tonight Show memorabilia and enjoy clips, games, and live shows.

There are also seating areas. Once you are called, you collect your 3D glasses. These waiting rooms are much better than standing in a standard line.

Then, board a "flying theater" and enjoy a race "through the streets and skies of The Big Apple, encountering everything from iconic landmarks to the deepest subway tunnels."

Dining

Finnegan's Bar and Grill – Table Service. Accepts Universal Dining Plan. Serves salads, sandwiches, fish and chips, chicken, corned beef, salmon, and more. Entrées are $15 to $25. This is our favorite place to eat in this theme park outside of Diagon Alley.
Louie's Italian Restaurant – Quick Service. Accepts Universal Dining Plan. Serves pasta, whole pizzas and slices. Entrées are $9 to $15. Whole pizzas are $35 to $40.
Starbucks and Ben & Jerry's – Quick Service/Snacks. Food and drinks are $3 to $6 each.

World Expo

MEN IN BLACK: Alien Attack

At *Men In Black*, your mission is to protect the city and defeat the attacking aliens.

You are sent in teams of six in vehicles and, using hand-held laser gundsas, compete against another group of riders to defeat the aliens and get a high-score.

This ride is a fun, family-friendly experience that we highly recommend. A Single Rider line is available.

Yes 📷 Yes 🔒 Yes 📏 42" 🕐 5 mins ⏳ Less than 45 mins

Children between 42" and 48" must be accompanied by a supervising companion.

Top Tip: Hold down the trigger throughout the ride. You get points for doing this, regardless of whether you hit any targets or not.

Top Tip 2: For major points, shoot Frank the Pug who is hidden on the ride in the newspaper stand on the right side of the second room.

Fear Factor Live

Get ready to watch theme park guests face their fears live on stage as they compete against each other in *Fear Factor Live*. This is a fun show that unites the crowds together.

Alternatively, why not apply and be one of those guests? To participate in the show, you should be near the entrance 60 to 90 minutes before showtime. Guests must be over 18, have photo ID on them and be in good physical condition to participate.

Volunteers are also chosen to play minor roles during the show.

📷 Yes 📷 No 🔒 No 📏 N/A 🕐 20 mins ⏳ None

We feel this show is starting to show its age, and we expect it to be replaced in the coming years by a new attraction, but for the moment it's a fun distraction - especially if you have never seen it before.

Hollywood

Universal's Horror Make Up Show

Go behind the scenes and see how gore and horror effects are created for Hollywood movies in this fun and educational show that is sure to have you in stitches.

The script is very well thought out, with laugh after laugh, and some fun audience interaction too. This is one show we highly recommend you visit!

The theatre is relatively small, so do get there early.

Yes No No N/A 25 mins None

If you want to be part of the show, the hosts tend to choose young women in the middle section of the theater. They also tend to go for someone who they think will speak little or no English, for comedic effect.

The Bourne Stuntacular

The Bourne Stuntacular will debut at Universal Studios Florida in 2020. Universal says: "This cutting-edge live-action stunt show based on Universal Pictures' blockbuster Bourne film franchise will blur the lines between stage and cinema in a hybrid form of entertainment that has never been seen before."

"Everything fans have come to expect from the action-packed Bourne film franchise will happen right in front of guests with live performers, high-tech props and an immense LED screen, making it impossible to discern where the live action ends and the cinema begins."

Dining

Mel's Drive-In – Quick Service. Serves burgers, chicken fingers, and milkshakes. Accepts Universal Dining Plan. Entrées are $11 to $16.50.
Schwab's Pharmacy – Snacks. Serves ice cream priced between $3 and 9.
TODAY Cafe – Quick Service. Serves sandwiches, pastries, and salads. Accepts Universal Dining Plan. Entrées are $9 to $14, pastries are $3-$5.50.

Springfield: Home of The Simpsons

There are many photo opportunities here, including a giant Lard Lad donut sculpture, Chief Wiggum by his police car, a statue of Jebediah Springfield, Duff Man flexing his muscles and more. Simpsons characters often meet in this area, and there are carnival games you can pay to play.

The Simpsons Ride

The Simpsons Ride brings the famous yellow Springfield family to life in a fun-filled simulated roller coaster ride in front of an enormous screen in Krustyland.

Your adventure is filled with gags throughout and is a fun family experience. Simpsons fans will love this ride!

Children between 40" and 48" must be accompanied by a supervising companion.

Yes | No | No | 40" | 6 mins | 20 to 40 mins

Fun fact: During the pre-show video, look out for the DeLorean car and Doc Brown from Back to the Future. This is a tribute to the Back to the Future attraction that previously occupied the same building.

Kang and Kodos' Twirl 'N' Hurl

This is a relatively standard fairground-style spinning ride, like Disney's Dumbo attraction. Here, you sit in flying saucers and spin around. A lever allows you

Yes | No | No | N/A | 1 min | Under 10 mins

to control the height of your saucer. Around the attraction there are pictures of Simpsons characters; when you fly past them, they speak.

Dining

Fast Food Boulevard – Quick Service. Accepts Universal Dining Plan. Despite looking like several separate Simpsons buildings, this is actually one area with the following sections:
- Moe's Tavern sells Buzz Cola, Flaming Moes and Duff Beer ($4 to $9)
- Lisa's Teahouse of Horror sells salads and wraps ($7 to $11)
- Luigi's sells personal-sized pizzas ($11 to $16.50)
- The Frying Dutchman sells fish-based dishes ($5 to $21.50)
- Cletus' Chicken Shack sells fried chicken and chicken sandwiches ($8 to $11)
- Krusty Burger sells burgers and hot dogs ($9.50 to $19)

Duff Brewery – Bar with snacks. Drinks are $4-$9, a hot dog is $10 and chips are $3.
Bumblebee Man's Tacos – Quick Service. Drinks are $4 to $8, tacos are $10.

San Francisco

Fast & Furious: Supercharged

Fast & Furious: Supercharged is a simulator-style attraction in which you take part in a simulated high-speed chase with the cast of the movies.

Fast & Furious operates a Virtual Line system. Instead of waiting in a traditional queue line, you make a free reservation to experience this ride using the Universal Orlando app or at kiosks by the attraction entrance. During quieter periods, you can simply walk right into the first show room. A Single Rider queue line is also available.

Theme park fans generally seem to agree that this is the worst ride in the park -

EX Yes 📷 No 🔒 No ▌40" ⊘ 5 mins ⧖ Under 15 mins

perhaps you can consider it something to do when it is wet, or if the waits for other rides are too long.

Fans of the franchise will likely enjoy seeing some

race cars up close and some familiar faces on screen.

Children between 40" and 48" must be accompanied by a supervising companion.

Dining

Richter's Burger Co. – Quick Service. Accepts Universal Dining Plan. Serves burgers, salads, and chicken sandwiches. Entrées are priced at $11.50 to $15.

Lombard's Seafood Grille – Table Service. Accepts Universal Dining Plan. Serves salads, sandwiches, catch of the day, mussels, and more. Entrées are priced at $16 to $27.

San Francisco Pastry Company – Snacks and Quick Service. Serves sandwiches, soups, and pastries. Accepts Universal Dining Plan. Entrées are priced at $5 to $14.

Woody Woodpecker's KidZone

This area of the park is dedicated to the younger members of the family.

E.T. Adventure

A cute ride where you sit on bicycles, like in *E.T.*, and soar through the sky while trying to keep E.T. safe. If you do not like heights, avoid this attraction.

It is a fun ride and one of the few Universal Studios Florida attractions that remains from the park's opening day.

Children between 34" and 48" must be accompanied by a supervising companion.

 Yes No  No | 34" ⊘ 5 mins ⧗ Under 20 mins

A Day in the Park with Barney

Join Barney and his friends for a fun-filled show where little ones can sing along.

 Yes No No | N/A ⊘ 15 mins ⧗ None

After the show, there is a play area, and you can meet Barney.

Animal Actors on Location!

A behind-the-scenes look at how animals are taught to act in films. Animal fans (and kids) will enjoy it, but we think the show is lackluster.

Yes No No | N/A ⊘ 20 mins ⧗ None

We would advise giving this a miss unless you are a big animal fan or you have time to fill.

Woody Woodpecker's Nuthouse Coaster

Think of *Woody Woodpecker's Nuthouse Coaster* as a kid's first coaster – a way to get them introduced into the world of coasters before trying something a bit more intense.

 Yes No No | 36" ⊘ 1 min ⧗ 15 to 30 mins

The ride is great fun for the little ones or just for those not wanting to jump on the likes of *The Incredible Hulk Coaster* just yet.

It is a short ride but should be more than enough to please young thrill-seekers.

Children between 36" and 48" must be accompanied by a supervising companion.

Dining

KidZone Pizza Company – Quick Service. Accepts Universal Dining Plan. Serves pizzas, pretzels, and corn dogs. Entrées are $11 to $14.50.

The Wizarding World of Harry Potter: Diagon Alley

The Wizarding World of Harry Potter may be the best-known area at Universal. It is split between the two parks: Diagon Alley is in Universal Studios Florida.

Shops

• **Quality Quidditch Supplies** – Sells apparel, hats and pendants, brooms, Golden Snitches, and Quaffles.

• **Weasleys' Wizard Wheezes** – Sells prank items, toys, novelty items & magic tricks, such as Extendable Ears and Decoy Detonators.

• **Madam Malkin's** – Find Hogwarts school uniforms, with ties, robes, scarves, and more. Also sells jewelry.

• **Ollivander's** (show and shop) – See a short show in which a wand picks a wizard. Then, buy your own.

• **Wiseacre's Wizarding Equipment** – Stocks a wide range of items from hourglasses to compasses, and telescopes to binoculars.

• **Wands by Gregorovitch** – The legendary wand shop.

• **Shutterbuttons** – Get a personalized "moving picture" like the Harry Potter newspapers for $89.95. Up to 4 people can take part in the experience. You are supplied with robes, but you must bring your own wand.

Interactive Wand Experiences

To participate, you must buy an interactive wand. These are $55; this is $6 more than the non-interactive wands.

Once you have a wand, look for one of the 25+ bronze medallions in The Wizarding World's streets that mark

locations you can cast spells. You also get a map of the sites included with each wand purchase.

When standing on a medallion, perform the correct spell: draw the shape of the spell in the air with

your wand and say the spell's name. Then, watch the magic happen.

This is a fun bit of extra entertainment, and wands can be reused on future visits.

Harry Potter and the Escape from Gringotts

Marvel at the fire-breathing dragon on the roof. Then, head inside and prepare for the experience of a lifetime.

The queue line is as much of an experience as the ride - you see Goblins, wizard vaults and even ride a huge elevator. The ride is a "multidimensional" rollercoaster-type attraction. It mixes real-world elements with 3D video on screens.

🎟 Yes 📷 Yes 🔒 Yes 42" ⏱ 5 mins ⧖ 30 to 60 mins

A Single Rider queue line is available, but it skips all the cool queue scenes.
Children between 42" and 48" must be accompanied by a supervising companion.

Ollivanders

Technically, this is a pre-show to a shop. You enter *Ollivanders* in groups. One person is chosen by the wand-master to find the right wand for them through the use of special effects in a short, interactive show.

 No No No | N/A ✓ 3 mins ⏳ Under 10 mins

When the right wand is found, they can buy it in the shop next door.

This is a fantastic experience that we highly recommend.

It is suitable for all ages.

The queue line at this *Ollivanders* moves much more quickly than the one at *Islands of Adventure*.

Kings Cross Station and the Hogwarts Express

Guests can break through the wall onto Platform 9 ¾, and catch the Hogwarts Express. This train ride transports you to *Hogsmeade* (in *Universal's Islands of Adventure*).

During the journey, you may see Hagrid on his motorcycle, the English

 Yes No No | N/A ✓ 5 mins ⏳ 15 to 45 mins

countryside, Buckbeak the Hippogriff, the purple Knightbus, the Weasley twins on brooms, and even some Dementors. The experience is different in each direction.

Once you hop off the train at Hogsmeade, you can explore the Harry Potter-themed attractions there.

Important: To experience the Hogwarts Express, you need a Park-to-Park ticket.

Dining
• **Leaky Cauldron** – Quick Service. Accepts Universal Dining Plan. Serves English fare such as Bangers and Mash, Toad in the Hole, and Fish and Chips. Breakfast entrées are $12 to $17. Lunch and dinner entrées are $10.50 to $22.
• **Florean Fortescue's Ice Cream** – Quick Service. Serves ice cream and treats, plus breakfast items & pastries. No Universal Dining Plan. Flavors include Earl Grey and Lavender, Clotted Cream, Butterbeer, & more. Ice creams are $6 to $8.50.

Park Entertainment

Universal's Superstar Parade
Expect to see The Minions and Gru from Despicable Me, Sponge Bob Squarepants, Dora the Explorer, characters from The Secret Life of Pets, and many others in the daily *Universal Superstar Parade*.

This parade is great fun for character fans. Both the floats and the characters are great to see, and the upbeat music adds to the fun.

This parade is much less crowded than the parades at Disney's theme parks. You

can usually get a front-row spot as the parade starts.

Having said this, although the parade is enjoyable, it is not up to the standards of a Disney parade. The parade is performed once daily; the time is on the park map.

Top Tip: Twice per day, before the parade starts, there are dance parties near Mel's Drive-In. During the dance parties, floats and characters from the parade come out to meet and greet, dance, and sign autographs.

Universal Orlando's Cinematic Celebration
Round off your evening at the park with Universal's nighttime spectacular. Presented on the theme park lagoon, this 20-minute-long show features scenes from Universal blockbuster movies, plus fountains, water projections, dramatic music, lasers, and pyrotechnics.

The ideal viewing area is from the dedicated area near Springfield, although the show is visible from around the lagoon.

Universal's Islands of Adventure

Universal's Islands of Adventure opened in 1999 with many famed attractions such as *The Incredible Hulk Coaster* and *The Amazing Adventures of Spider-Man*, which instantly put it on the world theme park map. The true revolution for the park, however, came with the opening of *The Wizarding World of Harry Potter: Hogsmeade* in 2010.

Expansion and innovation in the park have not stopped since *The Wizarding World* was unveiled. In this theme park, you will not find 'lands' or areas, but 'islands' instead. Together these islands make up *Universal's Islands of Adventure*. The park hosted 9.8 million guests in 2018.

Live Park Entertainment: There are no daily fireworks shows or parades. There are, however, character appearances throughout the various lands, in particular in Seuss Landing and Marvel Superhero Island. There are no Harry Potter characters in *Hogsmeade*, except for the Hogwarts Express Conductor.

Port of Entry

Port of Entry acts as an entranceway to the *Islands of Adventure* themselves.

To the right of the welcome arch at Port of Entry, you will find **Guest Services**. Here, you can get help with accessibility, dining reservations, as well as questions, positive feedback, and complaints. **Lost and Found** is also located here.

Lockers, a phone card vending machine and a payphone are all located to the left of the archway.

Strollers and wheelchair rentals can also be found here. **First Aid** is located inside the Open Arms Hotel building to the right of the entrance archway. There is another First Aid station in

The Lost Continent.

Fun fact: At stroller rentals, look for a sign with prices listing several gag items such as a gondola, an aero boat, and a rocket car.

Dining

Confisco Grille and Backwater Bar – Table Service. Accepts Universal Dining Plan. Serves wood-oven pizzas, sandwiches, pasta, and fajitas. Entrées are $13 to $24.
Croissant Moon Bakery – Quick Service. Accepts Universal Dining Plan. Serves continental breakfasts, sandwiches, paninis, cakes, and branded coffee. Entrées are $3 to $14.
Starbucks – Quick Service. Drinks are $3 to $6. Accepts Universal Dining Plan.

Marvel Super Hero Island

You will often find Marvel characters meeting guests in this area of the park.

The Amazing Adventures of Spider-Man

One of the most ground-breaking rides in the world, *The Amazing Adventures of Spider-Man* uses projections with real-world elements like never seen before as you swing around New York City with Spider-Man.

The storyline works well, the ride is fun and this is an absolute must-do.

This ride operates a Single Rider line, which can often save you a lot of time.

 Yes 📷 Yes 🔒 No | 40" ✓ 5 mins ⧗ 45 to 75 mins

The Incredible Hulk Coaster

Winner of numerous awards, *The Incredible Hulk Coaster* is our favorite roller coaster in Orlando. It is a truly outstanding thrill with huge loops, an underground

Yes 📷 Yes 🔒 Yes | 54" ✓ 2 mins ⧗ 30 to 90 mins

section, and non-stop fun from the moment you are launched out of the tunnel

until you are back.

There is a Single Rider line.

Doctor Doom's Fearfall

Doctor Doom needs your screams for power; to get them, he launches you into the air.

The ride features one high-

Yes 📷 No 🔒 No | 52" ✓ 1 min ⧗ 45 to 60 mins

speed launch up, followed by a free-fall down (and then up and down until you stop).

There is a Single Rider line.

Storm Force Accelatron

A standard teacup-style ride themed to Marvel superhero, Storm - and it's fast! An adult must accompany those under 48 inches (1.22m) tall.

Yes 📷 No 🔒 No | 48" ✓ 1 min ⧗ Under 10 mins

Dining

Captain America Diner – Quick Service. Accepts Universal Dining Plan. Serves cheeseburgers, chicken sandwiches, chicken fingers, and salads. Entrées are $11.50 to $19.
Cafe 4 – Quick Service. Accepts Universal Dining Plan. Serves pizza, pasta, sandwiches, and salads. Entrées are $10 to $17. Whole pizzas are $35 to $40. A Marvel Character Dinner runs Thursday to Sunday 5:00 pm to 7:00pm, and is $49 per adult & $25 per child.

Seuss Landing

This area is themed to the Dr. Seuss books. To make this land look unique, the theme park designers even made sure there were no straight lines anywhere.

One Fish, Two Fish, Red Fish, Blue Fish

A classic spinning ride, like Dumbo in the Disney parks. This one, however, packs a bit of a twist.

The soundtrack is actually a set of instructions you should follow to stay dry. So when you hear "up, up, up" you will want to steer yourself upwards and be as high as possible to avoid getting wet. This is a fun twist on what can be a bit of an unimaginative type of ride. At colder times, the water is turned off.

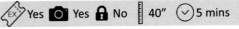
EX Yes | No | No | 48" | 90 secs | 15 to 45 mins

Children under 48" (1.22m) must ride with an adult.

The High in the Sky Seuss Trolley Train Ride

A cute, slow journey across the rooftops in Seuss Landing. The minimum height is 40" (1.02m) to ride accompanied, or 48" (1.22m) to ride alone.

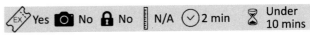
EX Yes | Yes | No | 40" | 5 mins | 15 to 45 mins

Caro-Seuss-el

A classic carousel type ride themed to the Seuss series of books. There is unlikely to be a wait for this ride at any time.

EX Yes | No | No | N/A | 2 min | Under 10 mins

The Cat in the Hat

Spin through the story of The Cat in the Hat. The ride makes more sense if you have read the books or seen the movies, but it is enjoyable for everyone.

EX Yes | No | No | 36" | 4 mins | 15 to 45 mins

Dining

Circus McGurkus Cafe Stoo-pendous – Quick Service. Accepts Universal Dining Plan. Serves pizza, pasta, salads, cheeseburgers, and chicken. Entrées are $9 to $16.

The Lost Continent

Themed to mythological creatures; home to the acclaimed restaurant Mythos.

Poseidon's Fury

A combination of a live show and walk-through experience with cool fire and water effects. Note that this show is standing room only.

In our opinion, this is a good watch but not worth more than a 30-minute wait. Return later in the day if the wait is long.

EX Yes | No | No | N/A | 15 mins | 15 to 45 mins

The Mystic Fountain

A witty, talking, interactive fountain in a courtyard area. You can ask the fountain questions and have a chat. The fountain also loves to tell jokes and to get people wet if they come too close! The Mystic Fountain only operates at select times of the day.

Dining

Mythos Restaurant – Table Service. Accepts Universal Dining Plan. Serves sandwiches, pad thai, salmon, and gnocchi bolognese. Entrées are $14 to $36. Only open for lunch.
Fire Eater's Grill – Quick Service. Accepts Universal Dining Plan. Serves hot dogs, chicken fingers, and salads. Entrées are $10 to $12. Large portions.

Skull Island

Skull Island: Reign of Kong

Step aboard one of the huge 72-seat 4x4 vehicles. Once onboard, each ride promises to be unique as one of five different drivers takes you on an adventure.

Universal puts it best: "You'll navigate perilous jungles, explore ancient temple structures, and encounter hostile natives – and that's only the beginning."

EX Yes | No | No | 36" | 6 mins | 30 to 60 mins

"Throughout the rest of your excursion, you'll brave foreboding caves crawling with prehistoric creatures, fend off unspeakable terrors – and even come face-to-face with the colossal Kong himself."

The animatronics, music, and atmosphere created here are second to none.

Single Rider is available.

Warning: The queue line for this ride is dark and there are actors in the queue line ("the natives") who scare guests as they wait. The ride may also be too intense for young children.

The Wizarding World of Harry Potter: Hogsmeade

Step into the world of Harry Potter and experience a visit to Hogsmeade. Dine, shop, and experience the wild rides. The area is incredibly themed and Potter fans will see authenticity unlike anywhere else.

Harry Potter and the Forbidden Journey

A truly ground-breaking ride featuring projections, flexible ride vehicles, and an incredibly detailed queue.

The opening of this attraction was a turning point in Universal Orlando's history, cementing its spot as one of the world's best theme park resorts.

The queue line of this attraction is an attraction unto itself, as you wind your way through Hogwarts Castle watching specially-crafted scenes and experience moments like the famous trio in the Potter books and movies.

At the end of the queue, it is time for an incredible adventure - this is a simulator-style attraction that blurs the lines between physical sets and on-screen projections. Plus, the moment your enchanted bench first takes off is breathtaking.

Yes | Yes | Yes | 48" | 5 mins | 30 to 60 mins

Expect to encounter dementors, take part in a quidditch match, come face to face with dragons, and much more.

There is a Single Rider queue line available, which can cut down wait times significantly; waits are usually about 50-75% shorter than the standard wait time in our experience, but this will vary.

Warning: We feel this ride creates mental strain due to the simulated sensations and the screens in front of you. This means that if you ride it more than once back-to-back, you may feel unwell.

Hidden Secret: When you are in Dumbledore's office hearing his speech, take a look at the books on the wall to the right of him. One of the books may do something very magical.

Flight of the Hippogriff

A small roller coaster where you soar on a Hippogriff and go past Hagrid's hut. Good

Yes | No | No | 36" | 1 min | 30 to 60 mins

family fun and a good starter coaster before putting your children on the likes of *The Hulk*.

Children between 36" and 48" must be accompanied by a supervising companion.

Hogsmeade Station and the Hogwarts Express

Catch the *Hogwarts Express*, and be transported through the countryside to Kings Cross Station (at *Universal Studios Florida*). The journey lasts several minutes, and as you look out of the windows, you will see stories

 Yes 📷 Yes 🔒 Yes 📏 48" ⌵ 5 mins ⏳ 30 to 60 mins

unfold.

Once you hop off the train at Kings Cross you will be by the London waterfront.

There, you can enter Diagon Alley for its attractions.

Important: You must have a Park-to-Park ticket to ride this attraction.

Hagrid's Magical Creatures Motorbike Adventure

This is *Islands of Adventure's* newest attraction - it opened in June 2019.

This family-friendly roller coaster launches you at speeds of up to 50 mph as you encounter magical creatures in the Forbidden Forest. You will go forward, backward, and drop - all as you ride a motorbike.

You have the option of either sitting on the bike itself or the sidecar. This ride is a fun and thrilling addition to the park and a must-do.

Yes 📷 Yes 🔒 Yes 📏 48" ⌵ 3 mins ⏳ 180-240 mins

A Single Rider line is available.

Shops

The shops are as much of the experience as the rides.

• **Filch's Emporium of Confiscated Goods** – The exit shop of *Forbidden Journey*. Sells apparel, mugs, photo frames, dark magic items, and trinkets.

• **Honeydukes** – Those with a sweet tooth will find love potion sweets, chocolate frogs (with collectible trading cards), and more.
• **The Owlery and Dervish & Banges** – Sells wands, Horcrux replicas, clothing, stationery, and even a

model of the Hogwarts Express.
• **The Owl Post** – A real post office where you can send letters or postcards with a Hogsmeade postmark and stamp. Stationery on sale.

Restaurants

The restaurants in Hogsmeade are well-themed, and the Quick Service food is some of the best in the park. We recommend you take a look inside these, even if you do not eat there.

• **Hog's Head** – Quick Service. No Universal Dining

Plan. This pub is located in the same building as Three Broomsticks. Serves alcoholic beer, non-alcoholic Butterbeer, and juices. Drinks are $3 to $9.

• **Three Broomsticks** – Quick Service. Accepts Universal Dining Plan. Serves breakfast meals. At

lunch and dinner, you will find Cornish pasties, fish & chips, shepherd's pie, smoked turkey legs, rotisserie chicken and spareribs. Entrées are $10 to $17. Family platters for 4 people are available for $60.

Jurassic Park

Since the Jurassic Park movie became a classic in 1993, children and adults alike have dreamed of visiting this incredible world of dinosaurs. Universal's Islands of Adventure allows those dreams to come true.

Jurassic Park River Adventure

On a boat, glide past enormous dinosaurs. However, this calm river adventure soon changes course. Watch out for the T-Rex before your 85-foot drop! A Single Rider line is available at this attraction.

Top Tip: The back row typically gets you less wet.

Note: Lockers are optional and cost $4 for 90 minutes of locker time.

EX: Yes | Yes | No | 42" | 5 mins | 45 to 90 mins

Camp Jurassic

A play area themed to the Jurassic Park movies. We definitely recommend exploring the area, as the detail is just incredible. This play area isn't only reserved for children. Anyone can explore the area, from the caves to the water jets and the treetop platforms to the slides.

Fun Fact: Step on the dinosaur footprints for a roaring sound.

Jurassic Park Discovery Center

An exploration area where you can see model dinosaurs, play dinosaur-themed carnival-style games, learn about DNA sequencing, and witness a dinosaur birth.

Pteranodon Flyers

Soar above Jurassic Park on a winged dinosaur glider. Guests over 56" must be accompanied by someone under 36" tall to ride.

EX: Yes | No | No | 36-56" | 1 min | 45 to 75 mins

Dining

The Burger Digs – Quick Service. Accepts Universal Dining Plan. Serves burgers, chicken tenders and chicken sandwiches. Entrées are $11 to $19.

Thunder Falls Terrace – Quick Service. Accepts Universal Dining Plan. Serves cheeseburgers, ribs, smoked turkey legs, wraps, and rotisserie chicken. Entrées are $11.50 to $20.50. The portion sizes are large.

Toon Lagoon

Toon Lagoon is an entire land dedicated to water – with two of the park's major water attractions here, as well as water elements everywhere.

Dudley Do-Right's Ripsaw Falls

Want a water ride that gets you absolutely soaked? Give this one a try.

The ride contains a well-themed interior and culminates in several drops with a final rollercoaster-style splashdown making sure you leave thoroughly drenched. The ride reaches a top speed of 45mph (over 70 km/h), so you get a great thrill!

A Single Rider queue line is available at this attraction.

Yes	Yes	Yes	44"	6 mins	60 to 90 mins

Optional lockers are $4 for 90 minutes.

Popeye & Bluto's Bilge-Rat Barges

Popeye's will make sure you come out drenched from head to toe. This is by far

Yes	No	Yes	42"	6 mins	45 to 90 mins

the wettest water ride at Universal, and it is a whole lot of fun! Universal has come up with creative ways to wet you. Optional lockers are available costing $4 for 90 minutes; the center of the raft has a covered section for basic water protection too.

Me Ship, The Olive

This is a kids' play area and a great place for a break from the crowds. For those who like causing chaos, there are free water cannons on the top level of the ship to spray guests on the *Popeye* water ride below.

Dining

Blondie's – Quick Service. Accepts Universal Dining Plan. Serves sandwiches, made to order subs and hot dogs. Entrées are $13.50 to $16.

Comic Strip Cafe – Quick Service. Accepts Universal Dining Plan. Serves Chinese beef and broccoli, chilidogs, sandwiches, fish & chips, pizza, and spaghetti and meatballs. Entrées are $10.50 to $19.50.

Wimpy's - Quick Service. Accepts Universal Dining Plan. Serves burgers at $11.50 to $19.

Volcano Bay

Volcano Bay is Universal Orlando's newest major addition - a water park based around an enormous, 200-foot-tall volcano - Krakatau.

Transportation

Universal Orlando is in a unique situation where it is landlocked on all four sides and therefore has to be creative about its use of land. As such, Volcano Bay is located on a small parcel of land next to Cabana Bay Beach Resort.

Volcano Bay does not have a dedicated parking lot, so guests staying off-site park at the Universal parking garages they do for the theme parks and catch a complimentary shuttle bus to Volcano Bay.

Guests of all on-site hotels (except Cabana Bay and Aventura Hotel) also have a complimentary shuttle bus from the hotel to the water park. Guests staying at Cabana Bay and Aventura Hotel can walk to Volcano Bay as it is right next door.

TapuTapu

Universal has revolutionized water parks with a park free from lines. You will need to wear a band called TapuTapu. It is given to you for day-use once inside Volcano Bay.

The TapuTapu allows you to:
• **TapTu Ride** - Attractions at Volcano Bay do not have standard queue lines. Instead, at ride entrances, there is a totem pole with a posted wait time. Tap your TapuTapu on the totem pole for a return time. Then, return to the ride entrance when your wristband vibrates. You will wait 5 to 10 minutes to ride (at peak times, it can be up to 30 minutes). You can only virtually queue for one attraction at a time.
• **TapTu Play** - Tap your TapuTapu on interactive park elements, and actions are triggered such as a water spray onto the lazy river or lights inside a cave.
• **TapTu Pay** - Using the Universal Orlando app, link your park tickets and TapuTapu to a payment card and use your wearable to pay. You can also set spending limits and a PIN.
• **TapTu Snap** - There are framed photo spots, tap your TapuTapu and pose. On-ride photos can also be added. Photos appear on the Universal Orlando app where you can buy full-quality versions.
• **TapTu Lock** - Use your TapuTapu to unlock your park locker (extra charge) - you can assign up to 4 wristbands to one locker.

Attractions

For each attraction, we list minimum height requirements and maximum guest weight restrictions.

Krakatau:
At the heart of the park, you'll see the 200-foot-tall volcano, Krakatau. By day, you'll see its majestic waterfalls. And by night, the volcano illuminates with blazing lava.

Three body slides are at the rear of the volcano; each starts with a drop trap door:
• *Ko'okiri Body Plunge:* (48", 300 lbs) A racing, 70-degree drop that plummets 125-feet through Krakatau.
• *Kala and Ta Nui Serpentine Body Slides:* (48", 275 lbs) Two intertwining drop slides where you'll fall freely along 124 twisting feet. Green is more intense than blue.
• *Punga Racers:* (42", 49" to ride alone, 150 lbs) A high-speed race through four different enclosed slides on manta-shaped mats.
• *Krakatau Aqua Coaster:* (42", 49" to ride alone, 700 lbs combined) The park's star attraction where you sit in canoes and travel up and down through the park's iconic volcano. A 4-person water roller coaster.

Wave Village:
Soak in the sun and relax on the sandy shores. Enjoy:
• *Waturi Beach:* (Under 48" must wear a life vest) A wave pool where you can swim, relax on the sand, or indulge in a cabana.
• *The Reef:* (Under 48" must wear a life vest) A leisure pool with calmer waters and views of riders on the *Ko'okiri Body Plunge.*

River Village:
River Village offers several family-friendly attractions and experiences:
• *Kopiko Wai Winding River:* (Under 48" must wear a life vest) A gentle, winding river through the volcano's hidden caves, featuring water effects and a journey through a starlit cave.
• *Tot Tiki Reef:* (Max 48") A toddler play area with spraying Maori fountains, slides, and a kid-size volcano.
• *Runamukka Reef:* (Max 54") A three-story water playground inspired by the coral reef.
• *Honu:* (48", 700 lbs combined) An adventurous, 2 to 5-passenger raft ride that soars across a dual wall.
• *Ika Moana:* (42", 49" to ride alone, 750 lbs combined) A twisting, group raft ride across bubbling geysers.

Rainforest Village:
Features an incredible assortment of attractions for thrill-seekers, including:
• *Maku:* (42", 49" to ride alone, 1050 lbs combined) A "saucer ride" sending 2 to 6-person rafts around three saucer-shaped curves.
• *Puihi:* (42", 49" to ride alone, 850 lbs combined) A 3 to 6-passenger raft ride that plunges you into darkness before bursting into a funnel and a zero-gravity drop.
• *Ohyah and Ohno Drop Slides:* (48") Two twisting, adrenaline-pumping slides that launch you four- or six-feet above the water at the end. Lifeguards will require to confirm you can swim as the end pool is 10ft deep.
• *TeAwa The Fearless River:* (42" with a lifevest, 49" to ride alone without a lifevest) An action-packed, racing torrent river where you ride in your inner tube amidst roaring, whitewater rapids.
• *Taniwha Tubes:* (42", 49" to ride alone, 300 lbs single or 450 lbs combined) Four unique slides with rafts for single or double riders.
• *Puka Uli Lagoon:* (Under 48" must wear life vest) A tranquil pool; relax.

Express Pass:
Guests with Express Pass access can access rides without reserving a time, but they must wait in the short queue once they enter each attraction. Express Pass is sold separately and it does sell out in advance - Express Passes cost $20 to $60 per person.

CityWalk

CityWalk is located just outside the theme parks and within walking distance of all the on-site hotels. There are shops, restaurants, bars, cinemas, and clubs.

CityWalk is Universal's free entertainment district, open from 11:00 am to 2:00 am.

CityWalk is often compared to Disney Springs, but this location is much smaller. CityWalk also has more of an adult feel to it, particularly at nighttime, when there is a focus on the club-like atmosphere. The shops and dining locations are also much more limited. It still, however, manages to keep a fun and friendly atmosphere no matter the time of day.

Parking is charged before 6:00 pm at the main Universal parking garages used for the theme parks. After 6:00 pm, parking is free.

Dining

CityWalk is filled with unique dining experiences. Prices quoted for entrées are for adult meals.

Quick Service:
• **Auntie Anne's Pretzel Rolls** – Serves soft pretzels. A pretzel and a drink combo is $6 to $8.
• **Bread Box Handcrafted Sandwiches** – Serves sandwiches and salads. Entrées are $9.50 to $13.
• **Burger King 'Whopper Bar'** – Serves burgers, wraps and sandwiches.
• **Cold Stone Creamery** – Serves ice cream: $5 to $10.
• **Cinnabon** – Serves cinnamon rolls and ice cream. Ice creams: $5-$9.50.
• **Fusion Bistro Sushi & Sake Bar** – Serves sushi and sake, and drinks.
• **Hot Dog Hall of Fame** – Serves hot dogs. Entrées are $7 to $18.
• **Menchie's Frozen Yogurt** – Serves frozen yogurt priced at $0.59 per ounce (28g).
• **Moe's Southwest Grill** – Serves burritos, tacos, fajitas and other southwest dishes. Entrées are $5 to $9.
• **Panda Express** – Serves Chinese food.
• **Starbucks Coffee** – Serves coffees, ice-based drinks, sandwiches and pastries. Drinks are $3 to $6.
• **Voodoo Donuts** – Serves donuts at $1.50 to $4.

Table Service:
• **Antojitos Authentic Mexican Food** – Serves Mexican-style food. Entrées are $13 to $31. Open for dinner only.
• **Bob Marley – A Tribute to Freedom** – Jamaican-style dishes. Entrées:$12- $19.
• **Bigfire** – Serves pasta, steaks, seafood, chicken and more cooked on an open fire. Entrées are $14 to $39.
• **Bubba Gump Shrimp Co** – Serves seafood and other dishes. Entrées: $12 to $29.
• **The Cowfish Sushi Burger Bar** – Serves burgers and sushi. Entrées: $10 to $28.
• **Hard Rock Cafe Orlando** – Serves burgers, steaks, ribs and other American-style food. Entrées are $12 to $40. Serves breakfast.
• **Jimmy Buffet's Margaritaville** – Floridian and Caribbean-inspired food. Entrées: $15 to $30.
• **NBC Sports Grill & Brew** – Sports-bar style setting with 100 TV screens. Serves salads & American-style

food. Entrées: $15 to $30.
• **Red Oven Pizza Bakery** – Pizza and salads from $11 to $16. Best pizza at Universal.
• **Pat O' Briens** – A music venue that serves New Orleans-style dishes. Entrées are $12 to $21.
• **The Toothsome Chocolate Emporium** – A steampunk chocolate factory with Table Service meals and mouth-watering desserts. Entrées: $11 to $30. Includes a take-out shake counter ($10-$14).
• **Vivo Italian Kitchen** – Serves Italian food. Entrées are $15 to $28.

Making Reservations:
To reserve Table Service restaurants, call (407) 224-3663 or visit opentable.com. Request Hard Rock Café Orlando priority seating online.

Movie Theater

CityWalk features *Universal Cinemark* with 20 screens. Adult tickets are $10-$12. Child tickets are $7-$9. Senior tickets are $8-$10. Additional charges for 3D movies of $4. Combine a standard movie ticket and a meal at select CityWalk restaurants for $28, including tax and gratuity.

Mini Golf

Hollywood Drive-In Golf is an adventure golf location with two different courses - one themed to sci-fi, the other themed to horror movies. The sounds, special effects, lighting, and theming truly immerse you in the miniature world you are in.

Tickets are $17 per adult and $15 per child (ages 3-9). An 18-hole-course takes 35-45 minutes to complete. Minigolf is open from 9:00 am to 2:00 am. Buy mini-golf tickets at least one day in advance at hollywooddriveingolf.com and save 10%.

Blue Man Group

The world-famous Blue Men create live music with makeshift instruments in a fun and hilarious musical adventure.

The show lasts 1 hour 45 minutes with no interval. There are between 1 and 3 shows per day, with shows starting between 3-9:00 pm.

Ticket prices vary on the day of the week. Prices do not include tax and are valid from Sunday to Thursday – add $10 per adult and $5 per child for Friday and Saturday shows. Higher prices during peak seasons.

Tickets can be bought at the box office, by calling 407-BLUEMAN or online at blueman.com.

Discounts for annual passholders, students with ID, and military members. Buying in advance online saves up to $10 per ticket.

	Tier 1	Tier 2	Poncho	Premium
Adult	$63.90	$79.88	$90.53	$106.50
Child	$28.76	$35.95	$45.27	$55.92

Nightlife

Bars and nightclubs include *Red Coconut Club, Pat O' Briens, CityWalk's Rising Star, the groove* and *Fat Tuesday*. You will also find music at *Hard Rock Live Orlando* and *Lone Palm Airport*.

If you want to party the night away, the $12 CityWalk Party Pass allows you unlimited one-night access to several locations.

Without a Party Pass, the cover charge for a single club is $7. *Hard Rock Café*

doesn't have a cover charge. Turn up before 9:00 pm to avoid most cover charges.

Multi-day tickets and Flextickets include a free Party Pass. Plus, Blue Man Show ticket holders get free CityWalk club access.

Shops

If you like shopping, there are plenty of places to visit including *Fossil, Fresh Produce, Quiet Flight Surf Shop, P!Q, The Island Clothing Store, and* a large *Universal Studios Store*. Finally, if you are in the mood for some ink, visit *Hart & Huntington Tattoo Company*.

Park Services

Universal Orlando offers a variety of services designed to ease your day, from photo services to Express Passes, and Single Rider queue lines to package delivery.

Ride Height Requirements

Many attractions at Universal Orlando have height requirements for guests' safety. We list all rides with height limits in ascending order.

No Minimum Height:
• Shrek 4-D - No handheld infants
• Storm Force Accelatron - An adult must accompany those under 48" (1.22m)
• One Fish, Two Fish, Red Fish, Blue Fish – Children under 48" (1.22m) must ride with an adult
• Despicable Me: Minion Mayhem in stationary seating

34" (0.87m)
• E.T. Adventure

36" (0.92m)
• Pteranodon Flyers – Guests over 56" must be joined by someone under 36".
• Woody Woodpecker's Nuthouse Coaster
• Flight of the Hippogriff
• The Cat in the Hat – 36" to ride with an adult, or 48" alone
• Skull Island: Reign of Kong

40" (1.02m)
• The Amazing Adventures of Spider-Man
• Despicable Me: Minion Mayhem to ride alone
•TRANSFORMERS: The Ride-3D
• The Simpsons Ride
• Race Through New York starring Jimmy Fallon
• The High in the Sky Seuss Trolley Train Ride – 40" to ride with an adult, or 48" alone
• Fast and Furious: Supercharged

42" (1.07m)
• MEN IN BLACK: Alien Attack
• Popeye & Bluto's Bilge-Rat Barges
• Jurassic Park River Adventure
• Harry Potter and the

Escape from Gringotts

44" (1.12m)
• Dudley Do-Right Ripsaw Falls

48" (1.22m)
• Revenge of the Mummy
• Harry Potter and the Forbidden Journey
• Hagrid's Magical Creatures Motorbike Adventure

51" (1.29m)
• Hollywood Rip Ride Rockit – Maximum of 79" (2.00m)

52" (1.32m)
• Doctor Doom's Fearfall

54" (1.37m)
• The Incredible Hulk Coaster

The Universal Orlando app

The Official Universal Orlando Resort App, available for free on smartphones, allows you to: access wait times for all attractions when inside the parks, get directions to attractions with step-by-step visual representations, see showtimes and special events, get custom wait time alerts, see park and resort maps, find guest amenities, see park hours, set showtime alerts, share on social media, and locate food items. You can even buy park tickets and Express Passes right in this app.

Ride Lockers

Many of the rides at Universal do not allow you to take your belongings onto them; loose articles must be placed in free ride lockers.

How to use the ride lockers:
• Go to a locker station. These are by all rides that require their use;
• Select 'Rent a locker' from the touch screen;
• Scan your park ticket to be assigned a locker; Keep this ticket with you on the ride to unlock the locker later.
• Go to the locker, put your belongings inside, and press the green button next to the locker to lock the door.

Some attractions use an old locker system, where you use your fingerprint instead of scanning your park ticket.

Small lockers are complimentary (14"w x 5.5" h x 16.9" d); these fit purses, wallets, cell phones, Potter wands, and drinks containers on their side. Larger lockers that fit a backpack or an upright drink are $2.

Small lockers are always free for at least the ride's posted wait time. For example, a 90-minute wait for *The Hulk* would typically allow you 120-150 minutes of locker rental time. If you keep your belongings in the lockers after the free period, it costs $3 for each extra 30 minutes, up to $20.

Water ride lockers are not free - they are $4 for a set period (the wait time plus a margin), and $3 for each extra 30 minutes, up to $20.

Top Tip 1: If your free locker time expires because the wait was longer than posted, speak to a Team Member.

Top Tip 2: Use another ride's locker instead of paying for a water ride one.

All-day park locker rentals: These are at the entrance to each park – they cost $10 per day for a standard locker or $12 for a larger locker. You may access these lockers as many times as you want throughout the day.

Meet the Characters

At Universal Orlando, there are many characters to meet, and they usually have little-to-no queues.

At Marvel Super Hero Island, you will usually find Captain America, Dr. Doom, The Green Goblin, Spider-Man, Storm, and Wolverine. They even make their appearances (and disappearances) on cool quad bikes most of the time.

You can also meet the Seuss characters at Seuss Landing, including Cat in the Hat, The Grinch, and Thing 1 and 2!

At Universal Studios Florida, you'll find The Simpsons characters including Bart, Lisa, Homer, Marge, Krusty the Clown & Sideshow Bob.

You will also find the Blues Brothers, the Men in Black, Shrek, Fiona and Donkey, Barney, SpongeBob, the Minions and Gru, and the Transformers characters outside their attractions.

Other characters also make appearances such as Scooby-Doo and Shaggy, Lucy Ball, Woody Woodpecker, Betty Boop, and Marilyn Monroe.

Character schedules are on your park map. Some are not listed and appear in Character Zones near the *Universal Studios Florida* park entrance, and in Toon Lagoon at *Islands of Adventure*.

Package Delivery

Universal Orlando's package delivery service allows you to purchase any item in the park and pick it up later and avoid carrying it all day.

You can choose to have your purchase sent to:

• **The front of the park** – The shop by each parks' exit turnstiles. Purchases made throughout the day are sent here for you to pick up. Allow 4 hours for delivery.
• **Your hotel room** – At on-site hotels, you can also have the package delivered to your room (or collection point at some hotels). It arrives the next day between 9:00 am and 4:00 pm. This is not offered the day before checkout or checkout day itself.

Universal Express Pass

Universal Express Pass allows you to enter a separate shorter queue line with much lower wait times. Express Passes are valid on all attractions at both parks, except *Ollivander's, Hagrid's Motorbike Adventure,* and *Pteranodon Flyers.*

At *Volcano Bay*, Express Pass allows you to skip the Virtual Line once per participating attraction. Hotel Unlimited Express Passes are not valid at *Volcano Bay*.

Express Pass costs $40 to $190 per person per day. The pass is free for guests staying at Hard Rock Hotel, Portofino Bay Hotel, and Royal Pacific Resort. Each person needs their own Express Pass.

How do I use it?
At a ride, show your Express Pass to the Team Member. They scan it, and you enter a separate queue line from regular guests. Waits are usually 15 minutes or less.

The 4 types of Express Pass:
• *Universal Express Pass*: One ride per attraction.
• *Universal Express Unlimited*: Unlimited rides on all attractions.
• *Park-To-Park Ticket +*

Universal Express Unlimited: Includes a park admission ticket for both parks and Universal Express Unlimited.
• *On-site Hotel Universal Express Unlimited Pass*: A perk for on-site hotel guests from the 3 most expensive hotels for everyone in the room for the whole stay, including check-in and check-out days. Unlimited rides on each attraction.

If you get an Express Pass, we recommend the 'Unlimited' versions.

Free Hotel Express Pass:
Guests staying at the Hard Rock Hotel, Portofino Bay Hotel or Royal Pacific Resort get free Express Pass. These are luxury resorts with fantastic amenities, queue-cutting is a bonus!

Example savings: One night at Royal Pacific Resort in the Holiday season for 2 adults is $494 including Hotel Unlimited Express Passes for your entire stay. Buying the Express Passes separately for these days costs $190 per person, per day. For two days, you would spend $760 on Express Passes. So, staying at the Royal Pacific Resort saves you over $250.

The price gets better with more people in the same room – with 4 people, you save $956 on Express Passes. It is cheaper to book a room, check-in, get your Express Passes and leave.

Do I need Express Pass?
During peak periods, an Express Pass is very helpful. It saves hours of waiting. However, Express Passes are very expensive. With careful planning, and by following our Touring Plans, you can do most rides without an Express Pass, even in peak seasons.

If you are visiting outside of peak times, school breaks and holidays, an Express Pass is not as useful.

If you can't afford them, skip the Express Passes and follow our touring plans – you *will* wait, but save hundreds of dollars too.

Child Swap

Sometimes, two adults want to ride an attraction but have a child that is not tall enough. Universal Orlando's solution allows you to take turns riding, but only queue once – Child Swap.

Simply ask a Team Member at an attraction entrance to

use Child Swap. Generally, one or more adults (Group 1) go in the standard queue line while another adult (Group 2) is directed to a child swap waiting area.

Once Group 1 has ridden the attraction, they go to the Child Swap area. Here Group

1 stays with the child, and Group 2 rides without having to wait in the queue.

This procedure varies between attractions and can be combined with Express Pass – ask Team Members about the specific procedure.

My Universal Photos

My Universal Photos is a photo collection system that allows you to get all your in-park photos in one place.

You can get a My Universal Photos card from any in-park photographer. Each time you take a photo, hand the photographer this card - they will scan it, and your photos will be linked.

Before the end of the day, visit one of the My Universal Photos stores where you can choose the best pictures and have them printed.

You will need a new My Universal Photos card for each day of your vacation unless you purchase a Photo Package. All in-park photos are deleted at the end of the operating day.

My Universal Photos Photo Package:
Pre-pay for all your in-park

photos. When you buy the Photo Package, you get two My Universal Photos cards. Scan either any time you have your picture taken in the park. These photos are uploaded to the My Universal Photos website, where you can later download them.

The package includes on-ride photos, character photos, and park photos!

To get a Photo Package, visit the My Universal Photos stores near park entrances. Alternatively, after riding an attraction with an on-ride photo, visit the ride's photo desk.

Photo Package Pricing:
• One day – $69.99 - sold online only
• Three consecutive days – $89.99 online & $99.99 in-park
• Fourteen consecutive days

– $139.99 - sold online only
• Shutterbutton's Photo Package – $139.99 online
• 1-Day Photo Package At Volcano Bay – $39.99 online, and $49.99 in-park

For most visitors, the 3-day package is the best value.

Top Tip: To buy Photo Packages before you go, visit presale.amazingpictures.com/UniversalFlorida.aspx.

Single Rider

Use the Single Rider line instead of the regular standby line to save time. This is an entirely separate queue that is used to fill free spaces on ride vehicles with guests riding alone.

E.g., if a ride vehicle can seat 8 people and a group of 4 turns up, followed by a group of 3, then a Single Rider will fill the free space on the ride. This makes the wait times shorter for everyone as every

space is filled.

Single Rider Lines can close if they become full, the park is too empty or if the wait is longer than the regular line.

Some rides have Single Rider lines that are not advertised - ask at attraction entrances if the Single Rider line is open. If it is, you will be directed. One example of this is the *Harry Potter and the Forbidden Journey* Single

Rider line, which is easy to miss.

If you are traveling as a group, you can use Single Rider – you will ride separately from the others in your party, but you can still meet up after riding.

Single Rider lines are available on at many major attractions.

Money Saving Tips

Take Food & Rain Gear
Bring your own food into the parks. Whether it is a bar of chocolate or a drink, you can get these items at a fraction of the price outside. Also, bring rain protection from home to avoid inflated in-park prices.

Buy Tickets in Advance
Do not buy tickets at the gate – you will waste time and pay more. Save at least $20 per multi-day ticket by pre-purchasing them.

You don't NEED Express Pass
By following our Touring Plans, you can see the majority of both parks in two days. If you want to do everything in one day, Express Passes are a must.

If you want Express Passes, stay on-site

On-site hotels are more expensive than those off-site, but staying at select on-site hotels gets you Express Passes for everyone in the room for the duration of your stay, including check-in and check-out days.

Express Passes are included in rooms at the Hard Rock Hotel, Royal Pacific Resort, and Portofino Bay Resort.

Stay Off-site
If you are on a budget, then stay off-site. There are many hotels just off Universal Orlando Resort property – a quick drive or walk. These rooms can cost a fraction of the price of the on-site hotels. Plus, many do not have a parking fee.

Loyalty Cards
AAA members, American

Express Cardholders, and UK-based AA members all receive discounts throughout the resort. The AAA/AA discount is usually 10% at restaurants.

Free lockers
Universal charges for lockers on water rides but not on any other rides. Simply, walk to a non-water ride and use those lockers, but do be prepared to walk a lot to save a few dollars.

Early Park Admission

During most of the year, Universal Orlando Resort offers one-hour early entry to one of the two theme parks, plus Volcano Bay. This benefit is available to on-site hotel guests and guests who have booked a Universal Vacation Package.

At Islands of Adventure you can access *The Wizarding World of Harry Potter: Hogsmeade* and the rides (except *Hogwarts Express*) and *Caro-Seuss-el.*

At Universal Studios Florida, you can access *The Wizarding World of Harry Potter: Diagon Alley* and its attractions, minus the *Hogwarts Express.*

Despicable Me: Minion Mayhem is also available.

During busier periods, both parks may be open early. Volcano Bay is open for early admission in addition to the theme park(s) - seven of the top slides are open.

How do I get Early Park Admission?
Guests staying at Universal on-site hotels show their room key to gain early admission to the parks.

Guests with a Universal Vacation Package staying off-site go to the Will Call kiosks by park entrances and enter a confirmation

number given when booking to redeem tickets with Early Park Admission.

Early entry is one hour before regular park opening – that is 8:00 am most of the year, and 7:00 am during peak seasons. Volcano Bay's Early Park Admission is usually at 8:00am or 9:00am.

Seasonal Events

Universal Orlando offers something different all year round. Whether it is live entertainment, horror mazes, or Holiday cheer, the team has it all covered.

Rock the Universe
Jan 24th & 25th, 2020
This is a whole weekend dedicated to Christian faith and worship.

As well as the main stage with Rock Christian acts, the FanZone has live music, band autograph sessions, karaoke, and more. On Saturday, guests enjoy the Candle-lighting Ceremony. There is also a Sunday Morning Worship Service. Select attractions operate.

This is a separately ticketed event. 2020 tickets are $72 for one night or $112 for both nights. Other ticket options are available.

Running Universal
Feb 1st and 2nd, 2020
This is the first Running Universal event. Here, you race around the parks for a distance of either 5km (3.1 miles) or 10km (6.2 miles). The cost is $72 for the 5km and $111 for the 10km, or you can combine park and race tickets. Racers receive a bag, a race bib, a race t-shirt, a medal, and more goodies. The minimum age for runners is 5 years old.

Mardi Gras
Feb 1st to Apr 2nd, 2020
Celebrate New Orleans with Universal's Mardi Gras.

The Mardi Gras Parade has colorful floats and incredible music. Enjoy the throwing of the beads from the floats. The Music Plaza stage hosts live acts on select nights.

There are also New Orleans Bands in the French Quarter Courtyard and stalls with local cuisine.

Halloween
Select nights from Sep 10th to Oct 31st, 2020
Halloween Horror Nights is an evening event with scare mazes (haunted houses), shows, and scare zones where "scare-actors" roam around frightening guests. The theming is second to none. Select attractions are also open during HHN.

The event "may be too intense for young children and is not recommended for children under the age of 13". No costumes or masks are allowed and there is no trick-or-treating here.

Halloween Horror Nights (HHN) is *very* popular, and Universal Studios Florida gets extremely crowded. In 2019, a single HHN ticket was $68 to $94. There are many options including adding HHN onto a daytime ticket, and multi-night tickets from $110. HHN Express Passes are $90-$160.

Holiday Season
Mid-Nov to Early Jan
The Holiday season at Universal Orlando is filled with fun and magic. The parks do not hold events for Thanksgiving apart from meals.

For Christmas, *Universal's Holiday Parade featuring*

Macy's rolls through the streets with floats from the Thanksgiving Day Parade in New York City daily. Mannheim Steamroller, the biggest selling Christmas band of all time, rocks the stage on select dates.

At Islands of Adventure, *Grinchmas Who-liday Spectacular* stars The Grinch retelling how he stole Christmas. You can also meet Dr. Seuss characters.

Hogsmeade and Diagon Alley have festive décor and entertainment. Plus, projections wrap Hogwarts castle in Holiday spirit.

New Year's Eve
31 Dec
CityWalk hosts live performances and a midnight champagne toast! The New Year's Eve party includes admission to clubs, party zones, a pyrotechnics display, food, a champagne toast, and more. Tickets are $120. Over 21s only. The theme parks are open late for New Year's Eve too.

Dining

When visiting Universal Orlando, you will find an abundance of food options, from standard theme park fare to fine dining.

Quick Service Universal Dining Plan

The Quick Service Universal Dining Plan is available to all guests and can be purchased at any theme park Quick Service location, at UniversalOrlando.com or dining reservation kiosks in the parks. It is accepted at over 100 locations throughout the resort.

Pricing
The cost of the Quick Service Dining Plan is $25.55 for adults and $17.03 per child. Prices include tax.

What is included?
Each day purchased on the Universal Quick Service Dining Plan entitles you to:
• 1 Quick Service meal

• 1 Snack
• 1 Non-Alcoholic Beverage

You will receive a voucher when you reserve your dining plan that is exchanged for a dining plan card at the park or *CityWalk*.

The Quick Service Dining Plan can be redeemed at most dining locations in the parks and some at *CityWalk*.

Is it worth the price?
In our opinion, the Quick Service plan is not a great purchase if you are looking for value for money. You have to try hard to profit from this dining plan by choosing the most

expensive entrées on the menu every time.

Moreover, we can't classify this as a real dining plan, as there is only one actual meal included – the rest, are drinks and snacks. This will likely not be enough for most people.

If, however, you want to pre-pay your meals to help manage your budget, you may enjoy this option.

Top Tip: Add a Coca-Cola Freestyle cup to this plan for $6 extra per day for unlimited soda refills for the day. More on these cups on the next page.

Universal Dining Plan

The Universal Dining Plan is only available to guests who have booked a vacation package – this includes both on-site and off-site hotels. The Universal Dining Plan cannot be purchased at the theme parks. The cost of the plan is $63.89 for adults and $24.48 for children (aged 3 to 9).

Each day on the Dining Plan entitles you to:
• 1 Table Service meal
• 1 Quick Service meal
• 1 Snack
• 1 Beverage

You can buy however many days' worth of credits you

need, so, it is possible to buy 3 days' worth of food during an 8-day stay. Credits are available for your entire stay.

Character fans can also use one Table Service credit for the Superstar Character Breakfast at Cafe La Bamba - worth $35.

The Universal Dining Plan can be redeemed at most locations in the parks and select *CityWalk* locations, but not at hotel restaurants.

Guests who purchase the Dining Plan receive a voucher when booking their

vacation to exchange in the parks or *CityWalk*.

Is it worth it?
If you like having all your meals pre-paid, and enjoy Table Service meals, then this is the perfect plan for you.

This plan generally offers better value than the Quick Service dining plan, especially if you eat the most expensive items on the menu, meaning that you can save money here.

Note: Gratuities are not included in the price of the Dining Plan.

Refillable Drinks and Popcorn

Popcorn:
Refillable popcorn buckets are a great snack for big eaters. You pay $9 for the popcorn bucket and then can get as many refills as you want for $2 each.

There are four places at each theme park where your souvenir bucket can be refilled. There are no popcorn refills at *CityWalk*, or the on-site hotels.

Popcorn refills are only available for regular popcorn; flavored popcorn is not discounted.

Coca Cola Freestyle:
Coca Cola Freestyle is a refillable drinks system.

You pay $17 for a Coca Cola Freestyle cup. Then, visit any of the 18 Coca Cola Freestyle locations and refill your cup for free as many times as you want that day. Additional days can be added for $10 per day.

You must wait 10 minutes between refills to discourage sharing.

Coke Freestyle stations at *CityWalk* and the hotels are not included.

Refillable Souvenir Cups:
Universal sells many souvenir cups in the form of characters (Minions, Simpsons) or themed (Butterbear cup). These cups cost around $17 each and are a nice souvenir.

Plus, you can visit most Quick Service and Snack locations at parks and get refills of sodas, slushies, and any non-specialty drink for $1.50. These cups are valid indefinitely so you can refill multiple times during your stay and even on future visits, perhaps.

For guests on multi-day visits who don't drink a lot of soda, the souvenir cups are likely to work out as better value than Freestyle.

Top 5 Restaurants

1. Mythos (Islands of Adventure) – This place is a pure delight to eat in, with its lavish interior, exotic menu, and rather fair prices. This restaurant will take you to a different world.

Entrées are $14 and $36. The food ranges from sandwiches to shortribs.

2. NBC Sports Grill & Brew (CityWalk) – Many ignore this restaurant when walking past, perhaps discounting it as tacky because of its sports theme. Do not be one of them; NBC Sports Grill has some great food on offer and the portions are large!

There is a wide selection of food on offer from wings to flatbreads, nachos, calamari, salads, burgers, pasta, steak, and more.

Entrées are $15 to $30.

3. Toothsome Chocolate Emporium (CityWalk) – Toothsome is an excellent choice no matter what you feel like eating. Plus, there are incredible milkshakes!

Entrées are $11 to $30. Food ranges from salads to burgers, pasta, salmon, and meatloaf. There is even a brunch menu featuring crepes, waffles, quiche, and french toast! Brunch items are $9 to $14 each.

4. Three Broomsticks (Islands of Adventure) – Everything about this restaurant puts it at the top spot: the atmosphere, the food, and the choice.

Breakfast entrées come from around the world: England, the USA, and Continental Europe.

Lunch and dinner revolve around British dishes with some American classics. You'll find Cornish pasties, fish & chips, shepherd's pie, as well as smoked turkey, rotisserie chicken, and ribs. Entrées are $10 to $17.

5. Croissant Moon Bakery (Islands of Adventure) – The food here is far from your standard theme park fare. This is a bakery and not somewhere to go for a full-blown lunch or dinner meal, but where you might go for breakfast or a snack.

Serves continental breakfasts, sandwiches, paninis, and great cakes! If you fancy a coffee, this is the place to visit too! Entrées are $3 to $14.

Touring Plans

To make the most of your time at the parks, we recommend you follow one of our touring plans; they are designed for you to see and do as much as possible.

How to use our Touring Plans

Our touring plans are designed to save you time which may mean crossing the park back and forth. You ride the most popular attractions at the start and end of the day when they are less busy. During the middle of the day, you visit attractions with consistent wait times, and watch shows to maximize your time.

Touring with Express Pass:
These touring plans presume you do not have an Express Pass. If you have this, explore the park in whatever order you want. *Hagrid's Magical Creatures Motorbike Adventure*, which at the time of publishing does not have Express Pass access, so do this first.

Without Express Pass:
Wait times can be long at both parks but you *can* do all the rides in one park in a day with some planning.

We recommend you spend at least one day at each park and use a third or fourth day to re-do your favorite attractions, as well as any you missed.

The key is to arrive at the park before it opens; that means being at the parking garages at least about 60 minutes before park opening if you are driving.

If you want to buy tickets on the day, be at the park 45 minutes before opening. If you already have tickets, be at the park gates at least 30 minutes before opening - the park regularly opens up to 30 minutes before the official opening time.

Using our Touring Plans:
Follow the steps in order. If there is a particular attraction you do not wish to experience, skip that step, and follow the next one - do not change the order of the steps.

1-Day Plan for Universal Studios Florida

If you have Early Entry, you should ride *Despicable Me* first, then explore the *Wizarding World*, then follow this plan.

Morning:
• Be at the turnstiles at least 30 minutes before the official park opening time.
• Ride *Despicable Me: Minion Mayhem*. If the wait is longer than 30 minutes, skip this ride.
• Ride *Hollywood Rip Ride Rockit*. Consider using the Single Rider queue line.
• Ride *TRANSFORMERS: The Ride*. Consider using the Single Rider queue line.
• Ride *Revenge of the Mummy*. A Single Rider line is available. We recommend the standard queue for the theming.
• Ride *The Simpsons Ride*.
• Ride *Men in Black: Alien Attack*. A Single Rider line is available; it moves quickly.

Afternoon:
• Have a Quick Service lunch to maximize your time.
• Watch *Universal's Superstar Parade*. You can get a good spot just minutes before it starts.
• Ride *E.T. Adventure*. Waits are usually less than 30 minutes.
• Watch *Universal's Horror Make-Up Show*. This is our favorite live show. Arrive about 20 minutes before.
• Experience *Race Through New York Starring Jimmy Fallon*.
• See *Shrek 4D*.

Evening:
• Experience *Fast and Furious: Supercharged*. Alternatively, watch *The Bourne: Stuntacular* - do both, if they are of interest.
• Head to *The Wizarding World of Harry Potter: Diagon Alley* at least 3 hours before park closing. Crowds are lightest at the end of the day. Ride *Harry Potter and the Escape from Gringotts*, then do a return journey on the *Hogwarts Express*. If you have time, experience *Ollivanders*.
• Watch the nighttime show on the park's lagoon to end your day.

1-Day Plan for Islands of Adventure

If you have Early Entry, explore the *Wizarding World*, then follow this plan.

Morning:
• Be at the turnstiles at least 30 minutes before the official park opening time.
• Ride *The Amazing Adventures of Spider-Man*.
• Ride *The Incredible Hulk Coaster*.
• Ride *Dr. Doom's Fearfall*.
• Choose between kids' rides or water rides for the rest of the morning.

Kids' Rides:
• Ride *The Cat in the Hat*.
• Ride *One Fish, Two Fish, Red Fish, Blue Fish*.
• Ride *The High in the Sky Seuss Trolley Train Ride*.
• Ride *Caro-seuss-el*.

Water Rides:

• Ride *Dudley's Do-Right's Ripsaw Falls*
• Ride *Popeye & Bluto's Bilge-Rat Barges*
• Ride *Jurassic Park River Adventure*.

Afternoon:
• Have a Quick Service meal.
• If you fit the limited ride requirements, ride *Pteranodon Flyer*s. This will be one of the longest waits of the day.
• Experience *Poseidon's Fury*.
• Ride *Skull Island: Reign of Kong*.
• If there are at least 4 hours until park closing, follow the next steps. If there are less than 4 hours, skip to the *Wizarding World*.
• Watch *Oh, the Stories You'll Hear*.
• Explore *Camp Jurassic*.

• Ride *Storm Force Accelatron*.

Evening:
• Head to *WWOHP*. Ride *Hagrid's Magical Creatures Motorbike Adventure*.
• Have dinner at Three Broomsticks.
• Experience *Ollivanders Wand Shop*. If you are also visiting Universal Studios Florida, skip this.
• Ride *Flight of the Hippogriff*.
• Ride *Harry Potter and the Forbidden Journey*. Get in line before the park closes.

Important: Queue lines shut at park closing. However, if the wait times are very long (1 hour+), queues may shut early. Ask Team Members if they expect to close early, especially at *Hagrid's*.

Best of Both Parks in 1-Day Touring Plan

You can't see all attractions at both parks in one day, so we only include the highlights in this fast-paced plan. You will need a Park-to-Park ticket.

Note: If you have Early Park Access, ride *Despicable Me*, then *Escape from Gringotts* first and then pick up from Step 1. If you want to ride the *Hogwarts Express*, do this at the end of the day.

Morning:
• Be at the turnstiles at least 30 minutes before the official park opening time.
• Ride *Hollywood Rip Ride Rockit*.
• Ride *TRANSFORMERS: The Ride*. Use Single Rider.

• If you did not have Early Park Admission, go to *WWOHP: Diagon Alley* and ride *Escape from Gringotts*.
• Ride *Revenge of the Mummy*.
• Have an early Lunch - we recommend Monsters' Cafe if staying at this park.

Afternoon:
• Go over to *Islands of Adventure*. Be prepared for long waits as this is the busiest point of the day.
• Ride *The Incredible Hulk Coaster*. Use Single Rider.
• Ride *The Amazing Adventures of Spider-Man*. Use the Single Rider line.
• If it is before 3:00pm, ride one of the water rides.
• *Explore WWOHP:*

Hogsmeade. Ride *Hagrid's Magical Creatures Motorbike Adventure*. This will likely be the longest wait of the day. Use Single Rider to save time.
• Ride *Harry Potter and the Forbidden Journey*.

If time remains, have dinner, or ride *Skull Island: Reign of Kong*. If you prefer more Potter, ride the *Hogwart's Express* instead.

Important: By leaving a major ride until the end of the day *(Forbidden Journey)* there is a risk that you may not be able to ride if it breaks down.

Walt Disney World Overview

Walt Disney opened Disneyland in California in 1955 – the park was a great success, but as Disneyland was built in a residential area, other hotels and shops started to surround the park with guests seeing billboards towering from inside the park and the illusion of an imaginary world was easily broken.

In the 1960s, Walt Disney developed his "Florida Project", a hugely expanded version of Disneyland. Disney began to secretly buy up 47 square miles of central Florida; this was the beginning of "Disney World".

Sadly, in 1966, Walt Disney passed away and the plans almost collapsed. Despite the loss of its founder, the company built Walt's dream, and in 1971 Magic Kingdom Park was unveiled. This park was based on Disneyland, but on a grander scale.

In 1982, Epcot became the second theme park. You can learn about the future, and visit pavilions representing the world's countries.

In 1989, Disney's Hollywood Studios became the third theme park – here, guests can experience rides and shows inspired by movies.

Finally, in 1998 the fourth theme park opened - Disney's Animal Kingdom Park - where guests can learn about animals, venture on a safari and go on wild rides.

As well as theme parks, Walt Disney World contains two water parks, golf and mini-golf courses, 30 Disney resort hotels, horse-riding areas, backstage tours, spas, shopping and entertainment districts and much more. It really is a Disney world.

You could spend several weeks at the Walt Disney World Resort; it is immense in scale and unimaginable until you experience it.

Getting to Walt Disney World from Orlando Airport

By Car - The total distance is 43 miles, and takes 45 to 50 minutes.
Shuttles - These small shared buses generally cost $25 per person one-way. Roundtrips are around $40. Mears Shuttles operate at the airport.
Taxis - These work out cheaper than shuttles for large groups (up to 9 people) and you get a private vehicle. Taxi fares are metered and about $65 to $90 to Disney World. An Uber/Lyft is about $35-$40.
Disney Magical Express - This is a complimentary service from MCO to Disney hotels exclusively to domestic and international Disney hotel guests. On the return journey, guests can even check-in for their flight at their hotel (selected airlines only).
Minnie Van - This is a private transfer run by Disney priced at $155 for up to 6 people.

Getting to Walt Disney World from Sanford Airport

By Car - The total distance is about 20-25 miles and takes 25-40 minutes.
Taxis - These work out cheaper than shuttles for large groups (up to 9 people) and you get a private vehicle. Taxi fares are metered and about $130 to $170 to Disney World. An Uber is about $60-$80.

Tickets

A basic ticket is called a **Base Ticket**. This allows entry into one park per day. You cannot change parks on the same day. **A Park Hopper** add-on allows you to change theme parks as many times as you want on any day. The **Park Hopper Plus** add-on allows you a number of entries into Disney's water parks, ESPN Wide World of Sports, a round of mini-golf, or a round of golf at Oak Trail family course.

Online Tickets

The official website to purchase Walt Disney World tickets from is disneyworld.disney.com. The online pricing can be seen below. Many online ticket resellers offer tickets at reduced prices. UnderCoverTourist.com, for example, has up to $65 off some Disney World tickets. We are not able to recommend any companies specifically.

	Base Ticket (Adult/Child)	Base Ticket + Park Hopper (Adult/Child)	Base Ticket + Park Hopper Plus (Adult/Child)
1 Day	$116-$169/$111-$164	$185-$239/$180-$233	$207-$260/$201-$255
2 Days	$226-$330/$216-$319	$306-$410/$295-$399	$327-$431/$317-$421
3 Days	$336-$476/$321-$461	$416-$556/$401-$541	$437-$577/$422-$562
4 Days	$435-$597/$416-$578	$525-$687/$507-$669	$547-$709/$528-$690
5 Days	$464-$631/$443-$611	$554-$721/$534-$701	$575-$743/$555-$723
6 Days	$478-$646/$457-$625	$568-$736/$547-$716	$590-$758/$569-$737
7 Days	$492-$662/$470-$640	$583-$752/$561-$730	$604-$773/$582-$752
8 Days	$518-$679/$496-$656	$609-$769/$586-$747	$630-$791/$607-$768
9 Days	$536-$691/$513-$669	$627-$782/$693-$759	$648-$804/$625-$781
10 Days	$554-$704/$530-$680	$644-$794/$620-$770	$666-$815/$642-$792

Prices above are for tickets purchased online or as part of a package through Disney combining a hotel and tickets, and are rounded to the nearest dollar. Ticket prices vary depending on a prediction of how busy the parks are during your stay. The busier the parks, the more expensive tickets are. Tax (of 6.5%) is included. Promotional tickets may be offered at other prices.

More Ticket Options

For tickets of at least 3 days in length, there is a discount of about $21 for online tickets versus the park prices - if you plan to buy at the park gates, add $21 to the prices above.

You can also buy park tickets at any Disney Store at the same prices as at the park.

Florida residents get discounts with a Floridian ID.

European residents have a few exclusive ticket options available such as Disney's Ultimate Tickets. A 7-day Ultimate ticket for 2020 is £399 per adult and £379 per child. A 14-day ticket is £419 and £399. Finally, a 21-day ticket is £439 and £419 respectively.

Ultimate Tickets give you unlimited entry into the theme parks, entertainment complexes, water parks, and mini-golf courses, and also include photos with Memory Maker.

There are often promotions offering a 14-day ticket for the price of a 7-Day ticket if staying at a Disney resort.

If you are planning on making multiple visits to the Walt Disney World Resort within one year, it can pay to purchase an annual pass.

Hotels

Having a place to relax after a long day in the parks is essential during a Walt Disney World visit. Thankfully, there are many accommodation options including over thirty official Disney-operated hotels and villas. These serve a wide range of budgets right in the heart of the magic.

As well as Disney's hotels, there are also partner hotels located on Walt Disney World property, but not run by Disney itself, and then there are hundreds of nearby hotels off-property. Central Florida is a hugely competitive market meaning some world-class luxury hotels are available, as well as many mid-range and budget options.

Disney's on-site hotels are split into four categories:
• **Value** - All Star Resorts (Music, Movies and Sport), Art of Animation, Pop Century and The Campsites at Fort Wilderness Resort
• **Moderate** - Caribbean Beach, Port Orleans (French Quarter and Riverside), Coronado Springs and The Cabins at Fort Wilderness Resort
• **Deluxe** - Animal Kingdom Lodge, Beach Club, BoardWalk Inn, Contemporary Resort, Grand Floridian Resort & Spa, Polynesian Village Resort, Wilderness Lodge, and Yacht Club.
• **Deluxe Villa** - Bay Lake Tower at Disney's Contemporary Resort, Boulder Ridge Villas at Wilderness Lodge, Animal Kingdom Villas (Jambo House and Kidani Village), Beach Club Villas, BoardWalk Villas, Old Key West Resort, Polynesian Villas & Bungalows, Saratoga Springs Resort & Spa, Disney's Riviera Resort, and The Villas at Disney's Grand Floridian Resort & Spa.

Generally speaking, the pricier hotels have more elaborate theming, more amenities and more transportation options. We highly recommend an on-site hotel for a Walt Disney World stay if you can justify the cost. Discover the extra advantages of staying on-site below.

Room prices vary by season. Prices are per night for a standard room with two adults, and include tax at 12.5% (unless stated) and exclude special offers.

On-Site Features and Amenities

• **MagicBands** with your room key, park tickets, meal vouchers, PhotoPass and more on a wearable bracelet.
• **Choice of Advanced check-in** and go direct to room option or standard at-resort check-in.
• **Laundry** facilities for $3 per load; dryers are $3 a load. Detergent: $1 per load.
• **In-room babysitting services** from $18 per hour at all resorts. The Dolphin Resort and Contemporary Resort also offer paid Children's Activity Centers and activities.

• **Entertainment at your hotel** - all hotels have an arcade and host outdoor nightly Disney movie screenings. Other activities at select Disney hotels include basketball, bike and boat rentals, carriage rides, golf courses, archery, fishing, golf cart rentals, jogging paths, gyms, pony rides, tennis courts and volleyball courts.
• **Late checkout** (subject to availability) at no extra cost.
• **No charge on calls** to Walt Disney World locations.
• **No charge for children under 17** staying in the same room as adults. In rooms with more than two adults, extra adults pay a supplement of $15 to $35 each per night.
• **A Disney shop** in each resort selling merchandise and basic items such as sunscreen.
• **Room occupancy** at Disney hotels is usually four people.
• A **24-hour front desk**.
• **Overnight self-parking** costs $13 at Value resorts, $19 at Moderates and $24 at Deluxes, per night.
• **Room service** in all rooms for a $3 delivery fee plus

18% gratuity.
- **At least one ATM** per resort.
- **Check in** is at 3:00pm and check out is at 11:00am for all resorts unless stated.
- All Disney resorts are **non-smoking** except in designated areas.
- **Room amenities** include cable TV, coffee and coffee-making facilities, a telephone, a table with two chairs, and an in-room safe.

An iron and ironing board are either in rooms or available at the front desk. Most standard rooms have two double beds or one king-size bed.

Exclusive Disney Hotel Advantages

- **Complimentary transportation** all across the resort, using buses, monorails, boats and Disney's Skyliner gondolas.
- **Extra Magic Hours**, allowing one hour's early entry into one theme park per day, and to stay up to two hours after park closing at another park.
- **Free parking** at the theme parks and water parks with your MagicBand.
- **Friendly** and helpful

Disney Cast Members
- **Free round-trip Magical Express** transportation to and from Orlando International Airport.
- **Complimentary in-room Wi-Fi** and at most public areas at resorts.
- **At least one pool**
- **Disney Dining Plans** available with package bookings – savings of up to 40% on meals.
- **A small refrigerator** in every room.

- **A refillable mug program** ($20) with unlimited drink refills at resort hotels for your stay.
- **Resort Airline Check In** – Check-in for flights directly from your resort, including checking in luggage and receive a boarding card. Available for both domestic and international passengers flying with: Alaska, American, Delta (domestic only), JetBlue, Southwest and United.

All Star Resorts

This 5840-room Value resort is actually three hotels located next to each other.

The All-Star resorts are the cheapest resort hotels at Walt Disney World. Note that there are no Table Service restaurants at these hotels - only food-courts.

Theming at these hotels is basic with large statues which are fun but will not transport you to a different place in the way that the premium resorts do.

These resorts offer a great-value stay for guests on a budget or who spend most of their time in the parks.

All-Star Movies - Five movie-themed buildings including one themed to

101 Dalmatians and another to Toy Story. Rooms have movie-themed touches. There are two pools. This is the most well-themed of the three All-Star resorts.

All-Star Sports - This was the first Value resort at Walt Disney World. There are three pools. A McDonalds is a 5-minute walk away.

All-Star Music – As well as standard rooms, there are family suites for up to 6 people with two bedrooms and bathrooms, two 27" TVs, a pullout sofa, and a microwave.

Location: Animal Kingdom resort area.
Theme: Movies, Music and Sports.

Transport: Buses – 10 to 15 minutes to Animal Kingdom Park, Epcot and Disney's Hollywood Studios, and 20 minutes to the water parks and Magic Kingdom.
Room Size and Prices:
$112-$245 for a standard room (260 ft²), $289-$547 at the All Star Music family suites (up to 520ft²).
Activities: Poolside movies & an arcade at each resort.

Pop Century Resort

This 2880-room Value resort is a step up from the All Stars.

Pop Century Resort is newer than the All Stars and given the slight increase in price we think this is worth the few extra dollars.

As well as the Everything Pop food court at this resort, guests are a short walk away from Disney's Art of Animation Resort and its variety of food options.

Location: Near ESPN Wide World of Sports.
Theme: Pop culture in the second half of the 20th century. See giant play doh sets, Disney characters, bowling pins, keyboards, 8 track tapes and more.
Transport: Skyliner to Hollywood Studios (15 mins) and Epcot (20 mins). Buses to all other locations.
Room Size and Prices: $154 to $316 for a standard room (260 ft²).
Activities: Three pools, a

playground, an arcade and a pop jet playground.
Extras: There is a 5000-square foot store.

Art of Animation

This is Disney's newest Value resort. It opened in 2012.

The theming and atmosphere at Art of Animation is vastly superior to the other Value resorts; the food court is also excellent.

Rooms at this resort are more expensive than both *All Star* and *Pop Century*, and most rooms here are family suites.

Standard rooms are very popular - you need to book

the suites are much more expensive.
Location: Near ESPN Wide World of Sports, connected to Pop Century resort.
Theme: Split up into four sections - The Little Mermaid, Finding Nemo, Cars and The Lion King.
Transport: Skyliner to Hollywood Studios (15 mins) and Epcot (20 mins). Buses to all other locations.
Number of Rooms: 864 standard rooms, 1120 family suites.
Room Size and Prices: Standard rooms are $180 to

$330 (260 ft²); suites are $428 to $771 (565 ft²).
Activities: Poolside activities, underwater pool speakers and an arcade.
Extras: The suites feature kitchenettes with a table, a master bedroom and three sleeping spaces.

Port Orleans

Port Orleans is a Moderate-level resort split into two smaller resorts - Riverside (2048 rooms) and French Quarter (1000 rooms).

Port Orleans is our favorite moderate resort: it has immersive theming, and great amenities.
The centerpiece of this resort is the Sassagoula River that flows towards the Disney Springs area.

Location: Disney Springs resort area.
Transport: Buses to all locations, plus boats to Disney Springs.
Room Size and Prices: $246 to $392 for a standard room (314 ft²).
Riverside Activities: Five pools, a spa and a kids' pool. There is also an evening carriage ride available. Catch-and-release pole fishing activities are

also available for $6 for 30 minutes. There is also a 2-hour fishing excursion priced from $235 to $270 for 5 people.
French Quarter Activities: A dragon water slide, a games room and a water playground by the pool. The pool is heated and has a Jacuzzi. Bike rentals are available.
Extras: Some rooms also have a trundle bed.

Coronado Springs Resort

This 1967-room moderate resort is themed to the Southwest of the US with Mexican influences.

Coronado Springs is a large resort and the only moderate-level resort to include a fitness center.

The centerpiece of the resort is a lake, surrounded by beaches with hammocks. The pool here is our favorite Moderate-level pool.

Location: Animal Kingdom resort area.
Transport: Buses to all locations. Hollywood Studios, Animal Kingdom and Epcot are 10 minutes away, and Blizzard Beach is 5 minutes. The furthest park is Magic Kingdom (20 mins).
Room Size and Prices: $223 to $372 for a standard room (314 ft²).
Activities: The main pool has a Mayan pyramid and water slide, with an

archaeology-themed play area. Surrey bike rentals. Every Wednesday, there is a Viva Coronado Springs Fiesta where guests can taste Mexican treats and take part in activities.
Extras: There is an air-conditioned 400-seat open-air-style market food court. There are 3 other restaurants. There are arcades, bars & a convention center.

Caribbean Beach Resort

This 2112-room moderate-level resort is themed to the Caribbean with large rooms for this price category.

We think this is one of the most relaxing resorts. There is a 45-acre lake in the middle of the resort. This resort is big and it can be a 15-minute walk or longer from the resort hub with dining locations to your room. This can be annoying

at the end of a long day in the parks.

This is the only moderate-level resort to offer rooms that sleep 5 people.

Location: Near Epcot, Disney's Hollywood Studios and the Disney Springs area.
Transport: Skyliner to Hollywood Studios (5 mins) and Epcot (15 mins). Buses to all other locations.
Room Size and Prices: $230

to $400 for a standard room (340 ft²). Pirate-themed rooms are $315 to $461.
Activities: Centertown has food courts, restaurants, shops, arcades, pools and a water slide. Bike and boat rentals. Four pools. Hammocks at no charge.
Extras: Pirate themed rooms are available at a surcharge. A two-hour Caribbean Pirate Adventure Cruise is available for kids ages 4-12 for $39 to $49.

Yacht Club Resort

The Yacht Club is a 630-room deluxe-level resort next to Epcot's World Showcase entrance.

The Yacht Club is one of our favorite resorts at Walt Disney World. The resort is right next to Epcot, and a boat ride away from Disney's Hollywood Studios.

The 3.5-million liter pool is the best at Walt Disney World and is shared with the Beach Club Resort.

The Yacht Club is a true deluxe resort and comes highly recommended.

Transport: Epcot is a 5-minute walk, or you can catch the boat from the dock at the back of the hotel. Hollywood Studios is a 20-minute boat ride, or a similar walk. You can reach Magic Kingdom, Animal Kingdom, the water parks and Disney Springs by bus.
Room Size and Prices: Standard rooms (380 ft²) cost $487 to $846.
Activities: Amazing pool with water jets, a water slide, a hot tub, cabana rentals, plus a quiet pool. Fantasia Gardens mini-golf is nearby. A volleyball court,

a gym, jogging paths & an arcade.
Extras: This hotel also has a clothes store and an in-house barber. Visit 'Beaches and Cream' and try to finish "The Kitchen Sink" sundae which includes a whole can of whipped cream!

Beach Club Resort

Located next to the Yacht Club, the Beach Club is a 585-room resort by Epcot's World Showcase entrance.

The Beach Club is twinned with the Yacht Club and comes equally highly recommended.

This resort feels slightly less busy than the Yacht Club next door, with fewer non-guests visiting.

Transport: Epcot is a 5-minute walk, or you can catch the boat from the dock. Hollywood Studios is a 20-minute boat ride or walk. There are buses to the Magic Kingdom, Animal Kingdom, water parks & Disney Springs.

Room Size and Prices: Standard rooms (380 ft^2) are $487 to $846. 1 bedroom villas cost $738 to $1179, and 2-bedroom villas are $1108 to $2026.

Activities: Pool with water jets, a water slide, a hot tub, cabana rentals and a quiet pool. Fantasia Gardens mini-golf is nearby. There is a volleyball court, a gym, a jogging track, an arcade, and tennis courts. There is a

scavenger hunt, and a Pirate activity ($55).

Extras: Buy swimwear and clothes, food, and souvenirs. Periwig's does haircuts. There are penny and quarter press machines and an ATM machine.

Boardwalk Inn Resort

The 378-room Boardwalk Inn is a fun resort with a unique 1920s and 1930s seaside charm theme. The resort is just steps from Epcot.

The Boardwalk Inn is one of Walt Disney World's more intimate resorts due to its small size.

Location: Between Epcot and Disney's Hollywood Studios, opposite the Yacht and Beach Club resorts.

Transport: It is a 5-minute walk to Epcot, although a boat service is also available. Disney's Hollywood Studios is a 20-minute walk, or a boat takes the same length of time. Bus transportation is available to the rest of Walt Disney World.

Room Size and Prices: $533 to $890 for a standard room (390 ft^2). The 1-Bedroom Boardwalk Villas are $738 and $1179, whereas the 2-Bedroom villas go for between $1108 and $2026.

Activities: There is a main pool with swimming tubes as well as two other pools, a

health club and a private spa. Bike rentals ($7 per hour). Also near Fantasia Gardens mini-golf.

Wilderness Lodge Resort

This 728-room deluxe hotel is just a short boat journey away from the Magic Kingdom. It immerses you into a turn-of-the-century National Park lodge.

Wilderness Lodge is one of our favorite themed resorts, as it feels like home from the moment you step inside. It is only minutes away from the Magic Kingdom, yet it feels a world away from the theme parks.

Transport: Buses to all parks; there is also a boat service to Magic Kingdom Park & Fort Wilderness resort.

Room Size and Prices: Standard rooms (340 ft^2) are $406 to $760. Deluxe villas are also available with 1-Bedrooms priced at $712 to $1185, and 2-Bedrooms at $1181 to $2157. Studio villas are also available.

Activities: Several pools, a water slide, two hot tubs, jogging paths, an arcade, boat and bike rentals, flag family, guided tours and a Hidden Mickey hunt. Character dining at Artist Point restaurant at dinner.

Extras: Concierge-level rooms are available.

Animal Kingdom Lodge Resort

This 1293-room African-themed resort extends the magic of Disney's Animal Kingdom Park with animals roaming the savanna just outside your window.

Animal Kingdom Lodge Resort is a magical place to stay at and is the closest thing you will get to experiencing a night in Africa while in Florida. The resort features three savannas, each with different animals and a distinct look and feel.

All rooms have balconies at this resort, but they do not all have views of the savannas and the animals - these cost at least $185 more than standard rooms. The smells from the animals do not reach the rooms, and they are well soundproofed.

You are welcome to explore all the savannas. A guide detailing where to find different species is available in all guest rooms.

Transport: Buses to all locations. An internal shuttle service operates.
Room Size and Prices: $417 to $705 in a standard room (344 ft^2). Jambo House and Kidani Village villas are $657 to $1158 for a 1-bedroom,

and $1051 to $2025 for a 2-bedroom.
Activities: Several pools and a fitness center.
Extras: There are savannah safari options for an extra charge. 'Dine with an Animal Specialist' event.

Grand Floridian Resort & Spa

The Victorian-themed Grand Floridian remains unmatched in splendor. This 900-room deluxe hotel offers 14 dining options.

"Pure opulence" is the best way to describe the Grand Floridian, but we find the hotel more "stuffy" than the others. If you like being waited on hand and foot, there is no better choice.

Location: By Magic Kingdom.
Transport: Monorail to the Magic Kingdom (and walking path being built).

For Epcot, change monorail lines at the TTC. Buses elsewhere.

Room Prices: Standard rooms are $710 to $1084. 1-Bedroom Villas are $972 to $1568, with 2-Bedroom Villas at $1577 to $2418. Standard rooms sleep 5 people and Dormer rooms sleep 4 people.
Activities: Arts and crafts, storytime, afternoon tea, Bibbidi Bobbidi Boutique, guided tour, princess promenade with Cinderella, character dining, silhouette

cut-outs ($15-$24), two pools – one with a slide and a play area, tennis courts, boat and cabana rentals, jogging track, volleyball, spa and gym, croquet and more.

Polynesian Village Resort

With its Hawaiian theme, and amazing location opposite Magic Kingdom Park, the 847-room Polynesian Village is our favorite deluxe resort.

The resort's theme is truly relaxing from the background music to the lobby, every detail counts. The beach here is one of the resort's best features.

You can lay on a hammock or a lounger and watch Magic Kingdom's fireworks.

You can also enjoy the resort's Torch Lighting Ceremony.

Transport: Monorail and boats to the Magic Kingdom. For Epcot, change monorails lines at the TTC.

Buses serve all other parks.

Room Size and Prices: Standard rooms (409 ft^2) are $593 to $973. Waterfront bungalows are $3009 to $5259.
Activities: A beach, water activities, two pools, a waterfall and water slide, a jogging path and gym. Boat rentals. Home to the amazingly-themed Trader

Contemporary Resort

Located a five-minute walk from Magic Kingdom Park, this 750-room hotel boasts large standard rooms at 436ft², great dining options and an ultra-modern theme.

The Contemporary Resort is strange: if you are looking for amazing theming, you need to look elsewhere, but if you want to be close to the Magic Kingdom, a deluxe resort and a lot of amenities, look no further.

Transport: Monorail to Magic Kingdom (or a 5-minute walk). Epcot by monorail and changing lines. Buses to other places.

Room Prices: Standard rooms are $498 to $829. Bay Lake Tower rooms are $591 to $964 for a studio, $861 to $1333 for a 1-Bedroom Villa and $1126 to $2300 for a 2-Bedroom Villa.

Activities: A gym, an arcade, basketball, volleyball, golf, and tennis courts. Water activities. Pool with cabana rentals. Pirate experience for kids ($55).

Extras: The Villas at Bay Lake Tower include studios,

1--and 2-bed apartments. California Grill offers some of the best food at Walt Disney World.

Fort Wilderness Resort & Campground

This resort has 788 campsites in the value range. The 409 cabins are in the moderate category.

At the most basic, you get a campsite to camp under the stars or in your RV with shared restrooms. If you love the outdoors, this is perfect. The Wilderness Cabins are a big step up and similar to a large Disney hotel rooms.

Location: A forest between the Magic Kingdom and Epcot.

Transport: This resort is in a 750-acre forest; there is an internal bus system. For the Magic Kingdom, there is a boat. Buses elsewhere.

Size and Prices: $84 to $228 per campsite (25' wide and vary from 25' to 65' in length), $400-$737 per cabin (504 ft²).

Activities: Horse and pony rides, a petting farm, bike rentals, a jogging trail, volleyball, basketball, shuffleboard, tetherball, and nature walks. *The Hoop Dee Doo Musical Revue* and

Mickey's Backyard BBQ dinner shows are great fun.

Old Key West Resort

This Deluxe Villa 709-room resort is themed to turn-of-the-century Key West.

Rooms are among the largest at Walt Disney World and the resort is also often discounted. It is a large resort which may be an inconvenience to guests - especially those using the Disney buses to get around.

Food options are limited. Disney Springs is a short boat ride away with many dining options.

Location: Between Epcot and Disney Springs.
Transport: Ferry to Disney Springs, buses elsewhere.
Room Size and Prices: Studio (376 ft²): $418-$663, 1-Bed (942 ft²): $569-$930,

2-Bed (1,333 ft²): $810-$1443. Grand Villas (2,022 ft²) are up to $2000.
Activities: Four pools, a white-sand beach, volleyball courts, watercraft rentals, a jogging trail, bike rentals, arcades, basketball courts, shuffleboard, a gym, tennis courts, air hockey, pool, darts, and bingo.

Saratoga Springs Resort

Saratoga Springs is in the Deluxe Villa category. This 1260-room resort is themed to Saratoga Springs in upstate New York.

Saratoga Springs is very similar to Old Key West, although this resort has slightly smaller rooms.

The Treehouse Villas are unique to this resort: they are 10 feet off the ground, offering great surrounding views and allowing you to feel immersed in nature - a truly unique experience.

Location: Disney Springs resort area.

Transport: Boats to Disney Springs. Buses elsewhere.

Room Size and Prices: Studio (355 ft²): $418-$663, 1-bedroom (714 ft²): $568-$932, 2-bedroom (1075 ft²): $809-$1438, 3-bedroom Treehouse villas (1074 ft²): $1016-$1798.

Activities: A pool with a water slide, spa, two whirlpools, an interactive

children's play area, an arcade, tennis courts and bicycle rentals. A full-service spa and health club.

Disney's Riviera Resort

Located in the Epcot resort area, this Deluxe Villa resort offers 489 rooms.

Discover Europe and the Mediterranean as Walt Disney did at this new resort - that's Disney's storyline. We don't feel there is very much of a European vibe here, personally.

As well as a fantastic rooftop restaurant, there are beautiful gardens, fountains two pools (including a quiet pool), and a gym.

The resort offers studio, 1-2-and-3-bedroom villas, but also a unique smaller 2-person 'Tower Studio' with many features such as the bed, microwave and fridge built into the wall.

Transport: Skyliner to Hollywood Studios (5-10 mins) and Epcot (15 mins). Buses elsewhere.

Room Prices: Tower Studios are $415 to $690. Deluxe Studios are $623 to $960. A 1-bedroom villa is $911 to $1415, a 2-bed is $1401 to $2149 and a 3-bed is $2808 to $4539.

Activities: A gym, giant chess set, two pools - one with a water slide, water play area, fire pit, character breakfast and signature dining, and a chocolate workshop ($60).

On-Site Non Disney Hotels

There are several hotels not run by Disney but on Disney property - most are near Disney Springs. Differences between these and Disney hotels include:

• No Extra Magic Hours (extended park hours), with a few exceptions.
• No Disney Dining Plans.
• Free bus transportation between the hotels and the theme parks (unless otherwise stated)- runs less often than Disney's services.

• No complimentary Disney Magical Express transfers
• Prices are generally lower than at Disney hotels
• Theming is largely non-existent.
• Some charge resort fees.
• Many are part of chains so you can earn and redeem loyalty points.

If you are interested in looking at these, the hotels are *Doubletree by Hilton Orlando - Disney Springs; Walt Disney World Swan and Dolphin Hotels; Shades of Green; Best Western Lake Buena Vista; Holiday Inn Orlando - Disney Springs; Four Seasons Orlando; Hilton Orlando Buena Vista Palace Disney Springs; Hilton Orlando Lake Buena Vista - Disney Springs; and B Resort & Spa.*

We recommend these on-site hotels over off-site hotels due to their location and transportation options.

Magic Kingdom Park

Disney's Magic Kingdom Park is the most visited theme park in the world with over 20.8 million visitors per year. Magic Kingdom Park was the first theme park built at the Walt Disney World Resort - it opened on October 1st, 1971.

Attraction Key

 Does it have Fastpass+?

 Is there an on-ride photo?

 Average wait time (on peak days)

 Minimum height (inches)

 Ride/Show Length

In the following sections, we list each attraction along with key info. To the left are what the symbols in the next sections mean.

Where you see the phrase 'DDP' this stands for 'Disney Dining Plan' - see page 104.

Main Street, U.S.A.

Main Street, U.S.A. is inspired by Walt Disney's home town of Marceline, Missouri and is themed to recreate a turn-of-the-20th-century street.

Main Street, U.S.A. features shops on both sides of the street and leads to Cinderella Castle at the end. From this 'hub' area in front of the castle, you can venture into one of six themed lands. Due to its location, you will walk along Main Street both when entering and exiting the park.

Main Street opens to guests approximately 1 hour before the official park opening time. This means you can enter Main Street and shops and dine before exploring the rest of the park. 5 minutes before the park's scheduled opening time, a show 'Let the Magic Begin' is performed in front of Cinderella Castle to officially open the park.

City Hall is on the left before

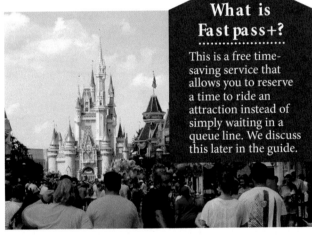

What is Fastpass+?

This is a free time-saving service that allows you to reserve a time to ride an attraction instead of simply waiting in a queue line. We discuss this later in the guide.

entering Main Street, U.S.A. This is the one-stop-shop for pins, badges, help, disability cards, positive feedback and complaints.

For shopping, the main store here is the huge **Emporium**, but there are many smaller niche stores too along both sides of the street.

The **Main Street Chamber of Commerce** is where you can pick up items that you buy during the day instead

of carrying them around the park.

In addition to the attractions listed here, you can enjoy the **Harmony Barber Shop** (a real barbershop - reservations are highly recommended at 407-W-DISNEY or disneyworld.com) and the **Main Street Vehicles**, which you can ride up and down Main Street, U.S.A. if you prefer to give your feet a rest.

Main Street U.S.A. Railroad Station (Suspended in 2020)

Hop aboard the *Walt Disney World Railroad* for a circular tour around Magic Kingdom Park on a classic steam locomotive.

The Railroad is a relaxing way to get around the park with several stations. At each of these stations you can get on or off - the other stations are located in Frontierland and Fantasyland.

The full tour of the park takes about 20 minutes, with trains every five minutes or so, but you are free to get on and off at whichever station

No | No | None | Up to 20 mins | Under 10 mins

you want. You can also stay on all the way around if you wish.

Note: This attraction is suspended for construction until sometime in 2021.

Town Square Theater

Fastpass+: Yes

Meet Mickey Mouse backstage at the Town Square Theater and create

memories that will last a lifetime. While you are at it, grab some photos too! Surprisingly, the queue lines are bearable with wait times

rarely above 30 minutes.

Other characters also meet at this location periodically.

Sorcerers of the Magic Kingdom

This is an interactive card game where you venture from land to land in the Magic Kingdom finding portals. Once at a portal, hold up your magic game cards and in-park screens will activate. Your cards will then help you defeat the Disney villains.

The more you play the game, the harder it gets, so you can progress throughout your trip.

To play, simply pick up your complimentary playing cards from the Firehouse on Main Street, U.S.A. Here you are given a map and full instructions.

This experience is included in your park admission at no extra charge and it is a great way to spend time in the parks without waiting in line. Guests can add five new random cards to add to their roster each day – the game is a collector's dream with over 70 cards to collect.

Dining

Casey's Corner - Quick Service, DDP accepted, entrées are $9.50-$13.50.
The Crystal Palace - Character Buffet, DDP accepted, $42 for adults and $27 for kids at breakfast; $55 per adult and $36 per child at lunch and dinner.
Main Street Bakery - Quick Service, DDP accepted, serves Starbucks products and bakery goods, sandwiches are $7, drinks are $3.50-$6.
Plaza Ice Cream Parlor - Snacks, No DDP, ice creams are $7-$7.50.
The Plaza Restaurant - Table Service, DDP accepted, entrées are $14-$18 at breakfast, and $17-$29 at lunch and dinner.
Tony's Town Square Restaurant - Table Service, DDP accepted, Italian food, entrées: $19-$36.

Frontierland

Step in and be transported to the old Wild West of the United States. As well as the attractions listed below, you can also explore the Tom Sawyer Island area on foot.

Big Thunder Mountain Railroad

Jump aboard a family roller coaster sure to bring a smile to everyone's face. This ride lasts about 4 minutes, which is unusually long for a roller coaster.

As you venture through the mine, you will see geysers, dynamite, western towns, caves, and more! This is a great family ride which is relatively tame as roller coasters go, and a way to get kids interested in something more exhilarating.

 Yes   No   40"   4 mins   90 to 120 mins

Splash Mountain

Splash Mountain is a log flume-style ride with a long indoor portion that follows the story of the Song of the South movie.

The ride is great fun with music, animatronics and small indoor drops to enjoy along the way – then, as the

 Yes   Yes   40"   7 mins   90 to 120 mins

action heats up, you plummet down a 52-foot drop at the end and discover why this is called Splash Mountain.

You do not usually get very

wet on this ride; it is more of a spray than a soak. However, there is always a chance you will come out drenched so leave your electronics and valuables with a non-rider.

Country Bear Jamboree

The Country Bear Jamboree is a sit-down theatre-show style attraction with pre-recorded singing from animatronic bears.

To be honest, it is probably our least favorite attraction in the Magic Kingdom as it is very outdated and has never resonated with us.

On the other hand, it does provide shelter from the rain and heat and allows for a sit-down break with no queue lines.

Dining
Golden Oak Outpost - Snacks, DDP accepted, nuggets and waffle fries are $6.50-$10
Pecos Bill Tall Tale Inn and Cafe - Quick Service, DDP accepted, entrées are $9.50-$15
Westward Ho - Snacks, DDP accepted, $9 for a corn dog, $3 for chips and $3-$5 for drinks

Liberty Square

Travel to colonial America in this unique land that cannot be found in any other Disney park around the world.

Haunted Mansion

Despite its name and its imposing facade, this is not a horror-maze or a horror ride – it is a gentle ride with tongue-in-cheek humor.

There are no jump scares but the spooky atmosphere and loud laughter may frighten young children, as well as the ghosts in the graveyard. It is also very dark inside. You will see dancing ghosts, singing busts, a ghostly seance, ravens and much more.

 Yes   Yes   None   8 mins   30 to 45 mins

The Hall of Presidents

This show features audio-animatronics of all 44 US presidents, as well as multimedia elements showcasing snippets of America's political history.

 No   No   None   22 mins   Until next show

Children, and those who are less politically minded, are unlikely to be entertained. However, patriots will likely enjoy the show.

The animatronics are incredibly advanced and are spookily life-like. The attraction features a speech from the current president.

Liberty Square Riverboat

Sail around Tom Sawyer Island on a leisurely cruise on the Liberty Square Riverboat. There is a very limited amount of seating and most space is standing room on this cruise.

No   No   None   13 mins   Until next boat

Closing times vary seasonally and a sign at the loading area will list the time of the day's last trip, as well

as the frequency of departures (usually every half hour).

Dining

Columbia Harbour House - Snacks and Quick Service, DDP accepted, entrées are $9-$16

The Diamond Horseshoe Revue - Table Service, DDP accepted. The all-you-can-eat family-style meal is $39 per adult and $21 per child. Entrees are $17-$22.

Liberty Tree Tavern - Table Service, DDP accepted, entrées are $20-$24 for lunch, and $39 for an all-you-can-eat family-style meal for adults and $21 for kids.

Liberty Square Market - Snacks, DDP accepted, hot dogs $8, turkey legs are $12.50

Sleepy Hollow - Snacks, DDP accepted, waffles are $7-$10.50, funnel cakes are $7, and drinks are $3.50-$5.50

Adventureland

Pirates of the Caribbean

Ahoy me hearties! Set sail through the world of the 'Pirates of the Caribbean'.

Featuring the characters from the famous "Pirates of the Caribbean" blockbusters, as well as original characters that inspired the hit movies, this is a fun water flume ride through pirate-filled scenes with a small drop to add a thrill element too.

Guests board boats and sail by scenes with amazing animatronic characters.

Well-known songs are played throughout the attraction adding to the

 Yes Yes | None ⊘ 8 mins ⧗ 20 to 45 mins

Pirate-like atmosphere.

The original version of this ride in Disneyland was the final attraction Walt Disney

supervised the creation, making this something truly special in the world of Disney theme parks.

The Magic Carpets of Aladdin

Hop aboard one of Aladdin's magic carpets and fly across Adventureland. This is a gentle ride and is very similar to Dumbo in Fantasyland.

Yes 📷 No | None ⊘ 2 mins ⧗ 10 to 30 mins

Swiss Family Treehouse

This elaborately themed walkthrough attraction allows you to climb up to the treehouse and venture from room to room seeing how the Swiss Family built their home following a shipwreck, making the most of nature around them.

There is no wait to explore this area and it is a good way to spend a few minutes.

Walt Disney's Enchanted Tiki Room

A Walt Disney original attraction, step into the frankly bewildering world of singing flowers and birds in the *Enchanted Tiki Room*. It is perhaps Walt Disney World's most bewildering attraction, and in our opinion is in need of a replacement for today's generation.

Located right next door to *Pirates of the Caribbean*, young guests can take part in **The Pirate's League** and be transformed into a pirate complete with make-up and accessories. Various packages are on offer and reservations can be made up to 180 days in advance at 407-WDW-STYLE or www.disneyworld.com. Prices are $40 to $100.

Jungle Cruise

Jump aboard and set sail through jungles across the world, with a skipper who just cannot help but tell the corniest jokes you have ever heard. Along the way you will see a variety of animatronic animals.

As each boat has its own skipper, the ride experience can vary from an outrageously hilarious trip to one where the guide offers minimal enthusiasm.

The queue line is fairly tedious with nothing much to see or do, so we

| Yes | No | None | 10 mins | 45 to 90 mins |

recommend you make a Fastpass+ reservation for this attraction.

A Pirate's Adventure: Treasures of the Seven Seas

This interactive game will have you exploring Adventureland looking for hidden treasures as you take on one of the five tasks dotted around the land.

When you begin, you will receive a magic talisman, as well as a map to help you along your way as you search for treasure.

Once you have found a spot,

touch your talisman and see how you change Adventureland around you.

Each mission lasts 15 to 20 minutes and it is a fun way to add a unique experience to your day without needing to wait in a queue line.

Top Tip: Complete 3 out of 5 missions and you will get a bonus FastPass+ for *Pirates of The Caribbean*.

Dining

Aloha Isle - Snacks, No DDP, dole whips and floats are $5-$7, drinks are $3.50-$4
Jungle Navigation Co., Ltd. Skipper Canteen - Table Service, DDP accepted, African, American, Asian and Latin cuisine, entrées are $19-$36
Sunshine Tree Terrace - Snacks, No DDP, desserts are $5-$7, drinks are $3.50-$4
Tortuga Tavern - Snacks and Quick Service, DDP accepted, American cuisine, entrées: $10.50-$15.

Fantasyland

Welcome to the place where you can let your imagination run wild in a world of Disney classics. Fantasyland is dedicated to the smaller members of the family.

Cinderella Castle

Step inside Cinderella's castle and walk through the entranceway across the moat and into Fantasyland.

Standing at 189 feet tall, Cinderella Castle is the central icon of the Magic Kingdom and indeed the whole of Walt Disney World.

As you cross the drawbridge and walk through the castle, be sure to look at the incredibly detailed mosaics around you.

Unlike some of the other Disney castles such as those at the Disneyland Resort and Disneyland Paris, you cannot visit the area inside the castle upstairs. The only exception is if you are dining at the **Cinderella's Royal Table** restaurant which includes appearances from the Disney princesses and select other characters.

Inside the castle on the first floor, you will find the **Bibbidi Bobbidi Boutique**, a makeover salon, where little girls can be transformed into princesses complete with make-up, a Disney costume dress and a hairdo.

Packages for Bibbidi Bobbidi Boutique vary between $65 and $450, plus tax, depending on what your princess chooses to do.

Boys can take part in the form of the rather reasonably priced "Knight Package" for $20 plus tax. It includes hairstyling with gel, confetti, as well as a sword and shield to keep. A deluxe package is $80.

Reservations can be made up to 180 days in advance by calling 407-WDW-STYLE or www.disneyworld.com.

Prince Charming Regal Carrousel

 No   No  None | 1 min 30 secs | Less than 10 mins

Ride a beautiful horse in the heart of the Magic Kingdom.

This is a beautiful vintage carousel, which pre-dates the Magic Kingdom and is now over 100 years old.

The carousel is fun to ride for every member of the family and wait times never seem to be more than 5 or 10 minutes.

For a different experience, visit the carousel at night and get to see it all lit up!

Note: This ride does not operate immediately before, during, or after any firework shows.

Mad Tea Party

A standard fairground ride where you ride in a teacup and spin.

If you want to go faster, just turn the wheel in the center of the cup – you can reach some dizzying speeds.

The wait times are never too long for this attraction and if the posted wait is anything more than 15 minutes, we recommend you simply come back later in the day.

Yes	No	None	1 min 30 secs	Less than 5 mins

Princess FairyTale Hall

Meet and greet Disney princesses in this most royal of settings.

Yes	Yes	None	1-2 mins	45 to 60 mins

Choose one of the two queue lines: one is to meet Cinderella and a visiting princess; the other is to meet Rapunzel and a visiting princess.

The interior of the meet and greet is lavish with stonewalls, chandeliers, and Cinderella themed stained-glass windows in the queue line. You will even get a chance to see Cinderella's glass slipper!

Please note that the ever-popular Anna and Elsa do not meet here, but at the Norway pavilion at Epcot.

Casey Jr. Splash 'N' Soak Station

This play area is a great place to cool down. There are streams of water from the giraffes and other animals and even a smoky mist from Casey Jr.'s chimney. As this is an open area, there is no wait to get in, making this the perfect place to let the young ones play.

"it's a small world"

One of the most memorable attractions, *"it's a small world"* features hundreds of singing dolls singing a catchy tune about the uniting of the world.

Your cruise travels leisurely

Yes	Yes	None	2 mins	30 to 90 mins

around scenes from across the world in this fun ride. The queue line for this ride moves very quickly.

This is a great Disney classic, which, although not based on any film franchise, is one of the many "must-dos" for most visitors.

The Barnstormer

A small roller coaster for kids with one drop and a few turns. The ride is good fun but it is very short, and rougher than it appears from the outside.

Yes	No	35"	1 min	25 to 45 mins

It is a good starter coaster for kids, and it has a very low minimum height limit

meaning that almost anyone of a suitable age can enjoy it.

Seven Dwarfs Mine Train

This fun roller coaster contains both inside dark ride elements and outside roller coaster sections taking you into the world of Snow White and even the Seven Dwarf's mine where "a million diamonds shine".

The ride cars swing as guests go around bends like real mine carts would. The thrill level is just below *Big Thunder Mountain* but a step up from *The Barnstormer*. It also fits perfectly in the middle for the height limit – a true family ride.

 Yes | Yes | 38" | 3 mins | 90 to 120 mins

Under the Sea - Journey of the Little Mermaid

Under the Sea is our favorite classic-style dark ride at Walt Disney World as it is perfectly executed.

The storytelling is great, the animatronics are amazing, the music is exceptional. The ride entertains throughout while moving slowly and steadily enough to not frighten young ones.

 Yes | No | None | 5 mins | 20 to 45 mins

Watch out for the incredible appearance of Ursula if you have any sensitive guests in your group, although the moment is quickly over.

Even the queue line is fun with incredible theming, character appearances from

Scuttle and an interactive game to play where you spot the crabs.

Top Tip: In the last hour of park operation, this attraction usually has no wait.

Mickey's PhilharMagic

Philharmagic is, in our opinion, by far Walt Disney World's best 4D show, and one that cannot be missed.

Here, you are attending Goofy's opera performance with Mickey's Philharmonic orchestra. When Donald gets involved, however, things get out of hand and

 Yes | No | None | 10 mins | Less than 15 mins

you end up on an adventure traveling through a world of Disney classic movies.

With an air-conditioned queue line and theater, shelter from the rain, and a fantastic movie, it is easy to

see why this attraction has one of the highest guest ratings at Magic Kingdom.

Top Tip: At the end of the show, Donald flies off the screen - look at the back of the theater for a surprise.

The Many Adventures of Winnie the Pooh

Hop inside one of Pooh's "hunny pots" and explore one of his many adventures.

This is a gentle ride where you venture through Pooh's stories; it includes slight

 Yes | No | None | 3 mins | 20 to 45 mins

rocking and jumping motions to enhance the experience.

As well as the popular characters, the ride is filled with bright colors that should excite the little ones.

Enchanted Tales with Belle

An interactive adventure where you are taken into Maurice's cottage, and are magically transported to the Beast's castle. Once there, you will meet Madame Wardrobe and have a chance to surprise Belle!

Not everyone in the group must take part in surprising Belle, but you can volunteer

 Yes Yes | None 15 mins ⏳ 30 to 60 mins

to help if you want. If you do not wish to, you can sit back and enjoy the show.

Even if you do not fancy meeting the princesses, we highly recommend visiting this attraction – it is definitely worth the wait and the attraction includes

some incredible special effects too.

Top Tip: Make sure you get a good view of the mirror behind the Cast Member at the start! The Lumière animatronic in the main show room is not to be missed either.

Peter Pan's Flight

Peter Pan's Flight is one of the Magic Kingdom's most popular rides. You board a flying pirate ship and take a voyage through the world of Peter Pan and Never Never Land.

The scenes are both beside you and below you, and the interior to this ride is stunning, from the moment you fly in.

 Yes No | None ⊙ 5 mins ⏳ 45 to 90 mins

This ride is incredibly popular, so a Fastpass+ reservation is a must.

The low ride capacity, plus the popular characters cause long waits to form. However, guests in the standby line can enjoy a fun interactive queue line that

takes you through the Darlings' nursery.

Note: If you are afraid of heights, this ride may not be suitable for you as the ships give the sensation of flight. At times, you are several feet off the ground.

Dumbo: The Flying Elephant

Dumbo is one of the most popular rides at Magic Kingdom Park. As you gently spin, use the lever at front of the seats in each Dumbo elephant to lift yourself up or down!

When you are in-flight, the ride offers nice views of the

 Yes No | None ⊙ 90 secs ⏳ 20 to 45 mins

surrounding area, as well as a whole lot of fun.

Due to its popularity, there are now two sets of Dumbos, and wait times are shorter than in the past.

Disney uses a clever waiting system where you are given a pager. Kids can play in a play area - once it is your turn to board, you are paged. You forget you are queuing!

Dining

Be Our Guest Restaurant - Quick Service [breakfast and lunch] and Table Service [2 credits - dinner], DDP accepted – the breakfast prix fixe meal is $29 for adults and $16 for children, lunch entrées are $15-$19, dinner prix fixe meals are $62 per adult and $37 per child. Reservations are required for all meals, including Quick Service.
Cheshire Café - Snacks, No DDP, Cheshire Cat tail snack - $5.50, drinks are $3.50-$5
Cinderella's Royal Table - Table Service, DDP accepted, breakfast prices are $62 per adult ($37 per child), lunch & dinner is $75 per adult and $4 per child.
Gaston's Tavern - Snacks, DDP accepted, snacks are $3.50-$10.50, & drinks are $3-$13
Pinocchio Village Haus - Snacks and Quick Service, DDP accepted, entrées are $10-$13.50.
Prince Eric's Village Market - Snacks, No DDP, snacks such as fruits & pretzels are $2-$10.
Storybook Treats - Snacks, No DDP, ice creams and floats are $5-$7.
The Friar's Nook - Quick Service, DDP accepted, entrees are $10-$11.

Tomorrowland

Have a taste of the future in this land that leaves today behind.

Buzz Lightyear's Space Ranger Spin

Buzz Lightyear invites you to step aboard his ship and use the on-board blasters to help defeat the evil emperor Zurg. By shooting the targets around you, you will be helping out Buzz and racking up points.

Different targets are worth different amounts of points and there are even hidden targets to get thousands of bonus points at once.

Yes	 Yes	None	5 mins	45 to 60 mins

You can also change the direction of your Space Cruiser with the joystick in the middle of the vehicle and turn the car the other way if you spot a target your friend has not. At the end of the ride, the one with the most points wins.

It is competitive and endlessly 're-rideable'. Great fun!

Tomorrowland Transit Authority Peoplemover

One of our favorite hidden gems at the Magic Kingdom is the *Peoplemover* - a relaxing way to tour Tomorrowland including seeing the inside of *Space Mountain* and *Buzz*

No	No	None	10 mins	Less than 15 mins

Lightyear Space Ranger Spin!

The ten-minute ride is a

chance to put up your feet. Wait times for the *Peoplemover* are usually just a few minutes.

Tomorrowland Speedway

Little kids are notorious for loving little cars and this is their first chance to have a go driving for themselves.

Yes	No	32"	5 mins	30 to 60 mins

Here, you get to cruise along at up to 7mph and enjoy the sights. It's great fun for car-obsessed kids!

The minimum height is 54" to drive alone, and kids must be at least 32" tall to ride with an adult.

Nearby photo kiosks let you

buy a *Tomorrowland Speedway* 'driving license' plastic card souvenir for $5.

Monsters, Inc. Laugh Floor

Step in for an interactive show with Mike Wazowski and his comical friends from 'Monsters Inc.' who are ready to interact with the audience, including you.

Yes	No	None	12 mins	15 to 30 mins

Get ready to laugh, play, and potentially be made fun of. Be sure to have fun or you

might have the pleasure of being dubbed by the monsters as "That Guy".

Space Mountain

Space Mountain is a roller coaster through space designed with the family in mind - it has no loops or inversions and provides the feeling of soaring through the galactic world.

This is not the wildest thrill ride in the world, but a fun adventure nonetheless - it is still the most intense coaster at the Magic Kingdom.

We strongly recommend making a Fastpass+ reservation as the standby queue line is slow moving and not one that you want

 Yes   Yes | 40"   3 mins ⧖ 90 to 120 mins

to be stuck in.

Alternatively, get to this ride

first thing in the morning or at the end of the day to minimize your wait.

Astro Orbiter

Above the *Peoplemover* is *Astro Orbiter*, a spinning type ride similar to *Dumbo The Flying Elephant* and *The Magic Carpets of Aladdin*.

The difference here, is that these rockets spin faster, and

 No   No | None   90 secs ⧖ 25 to 45 mins

you are much higher up – so high up, that you can see outside the park!

This is a fun ride but you

should know that the space rockets are very small and getting two adults into one is tough! Even an adult and a child is a tight fit.

Walt Disney's Carousel of Progress

A classic attraction designed by Walt Disney, the *Carousel of Progress* is a touching, funny and heartwarming show that moves from scene to scene every few minutes.

You start off seeing a family at the turn of the century and see how life was like in the early 1900s, then every

No No | None 20 mins ⧖ Less than 10 mins

few minutes the carousel rotates and you move forward in time with the family by a few decades.

There are some great in-jokes and it is fun to see how the year 2000 ('the

future') at the end was envisioned back in the 1960s.

As the song throughout the ride lets you know "There is a great big beautiful tomorrow just a dream away!"

Dining

Auntie Gravity's Galactic Goodies - Snacks, No DDP, ice creams are $5.50-$7, drinks: $3.50-$4
Cool Ship - Snacks, No DDP, drinks are $3-$5, a hot dog with chips is $9
Cosmic Ray's Starlight Café - Quick Service, DDP accepted, churros are $6.50
The Lunching Pad - Snacks and Quick Service, DDP accepted, entrées are $9.50-$13
Tomorrowland Terrace Restaurant - Snacks and Quick Service, DDP accepted, entrées are $10.50-$13

Live Entertainment

Magic Kingdom Park has plenty of entertainment throughout the day - all this is included with your park admission. The Times Guide provides you with timings - you can get this in the MyDisneyExperience app, at the park entrance, and most park shops.

Flag Retreat (Main Street, U.S.A.) – Hear patriotic songs as the American flag is lowered and folded in the afternoon each day with the help of a guest – usually a service person or a veteran. Length: About 15 minutes.

Citizens of Main Street – Meet the citizens of Main Street, U.S.A., including the Mayor, the chief fireman, and other locals.

Main Street Philharmonic at Main Street, U.S.A. – This band plays Disney tunes.

Main Street Trolley Show – A 5-minute show around a horse-drawn streetcar. This usually takes place several times in the morning.

Casey's Corner Pianist (Main Street, U.S.A.) – Join the pianist at Casey's Corner and listen to his tunes. He even takes song requests.

Main Street Philharmonic at Storybook Circus (Fantasyland) – This classic band plays tunes from Disney movies.

"A Totally Tomorrowland Christmas Show" (Tomorrowland – Holiday season only) – Join this intergalactic Christmas party where Stitch jets off to find Santa. Length: 20 minutes.

The Dapper Dans (Main Street, U.S.A.) – Enjoy the live singing from this barbershop quartet.

Stage Shows

Mickey's Royal Friendship Faire – This 20-minute show features Mickey Mouse and his friends, along with characters from some of Disney's newest classics.

A Frozen Holiday Wish (Holiday Season) – See Cinderella's Castle be transformed into a glittering, icy palace with the help of Anna and Elsa.

"Celebrate the Season" Show (Holiday season) – This 25-minute show features Mickey and Minnie as they spread some holiday cheer, including Disney songs.

Parades

Disney's Festival of Fantasy Parade is a must-watch; it is the park's main parade. It usually takes place at 2:00pm or 3:00pm daily and starts in Frontierland by *Splash Mountain*. It goes through Liberty Square, round the castle hub, and down Main Street, U.S.A.

The parade brings the magical stories of Fantasyland to life through parade floats, vibrant costumes, and an original soundtrack that features beloved songs from favorite

Disney films.

Ariel and friends grace a larger-than-life music box showcasing a musical party "Under the Sea", while Scottish dancers and a bagpipe-shaped float announce the arrival of Merida.

Other floats celebrate Disney Princesses and Dumbo; Peter Pan and Wendy soar above a pirate galleon; a steampunk Maleficent float makings a stunning entrance, and

Rapunzel and Flynn Rider appear too!

A Dining Package with reserved parade viewing is available at Tony's Town Square Restaurant. At the cost of $54 for adults and $19 for children (ages 3-9), the package provides an enjoyable way to combine a meal and some entertainment.

The Move It! Shake It! MousekeDance It! Street Party happens up to three times a day with the main show taking place on the hub in front of Cinderella Castle. In this interactive parade, the floats stop and you get to join in with the dancing.

During the Halloween season, you can see **Mickey's "Boo to You" Halloween Parade**, and during the Holiday season there is a special parade too, **Mickey's Once Upon a Christmastime Parade**.

Fireworks

Every evening, experience a grand finale to your day with spectacular fireworks in *Happily Ever After*.

Happily Ever After starts with a dream... and takes you on a journey that captures the heart, humor, and heroism of Disney animated movies.

This 18-minute show features more lasers, lights, and projections than any other spectacular in the Magic Kingdom's history!

Get a spot in front of the castle at least 45 minutes in advance. For the best view, you will want to be near Casey's Corner on Main Street, U.S.A - or anywhere in the hub in front of the castle. Get too close though, and you miss the fireworks behind the castle and cannot appreciate the projections.

The show can also be viewed from anywhere along Main Street, the Railroad Station at the park entrance, as well as from nearby hotels. You can also view the show from almost anywhere in the park but a key part of this show is the projections, so a view of the front of the castle is ideal.

Halloween-themed fireworks play during Disney's Halloween Season parties, and during the Christmas parties, you can enjoy festive fireworks. On the 3rd and 4th July you can enjoy *Disney's Celebrate America! – A Fourth of July Concert in the Sky* fireworks.

Fireworks Dessert Party
At Tomorrowland Terrace Restaurant, tempting desserts, fruits and cheeses await. As showtime nears, Cast Members escort you to a prime standing area in the Plaza Garden for viewing of the nighttime fireworks spectacular. Then, watch as the skies ignite and Cinderella Castle glows.

The Fireworks Dessert Party is $99 for adults and $59 for children, tax included.

Ferrytale Fireworks – A Sparkling Dessert Cruise
Sail on an iconic, double-stack ferryboat with delectable desserts inspired by the landmarks around you, as well as a fabulous fruit and cheese spread.

Enjoy this sweet ending to your day, before watching the fireworks. The show audio is piped through the boat's sound system for this magical viewing.

This experience is offered on select dates and costs $99 for adults and $69 for ages 3 to 9, including tax and gratuity.

Epcot

Epcot was the second theme park at Walt Disney World, opening in 1982. Its name is an acronym and stands for the 'Experimental Prototype Community of Tomorrow', Walt Disney's vision for the future of cities.

Although, Epcot never became a 'City of Tomorrow', today's version of Epcot is still one of the most unique concepts for a theme park anywhere in the world.

The park is split into two halves:
• **Future World** is where world-class attractions take you into the future and beyond. Here you can soar around the world on a paraglider, enter a futuristic test track and blast off into space.
• **World Showcase** is made up of Pavilions representing different countries. Here you are immersed into different cultures with food, attractions, architecture and more. Each person working at the pavilions has been recruited to work there for a year by Disney from their own country for an extra layer of authenticity.

The park is currently going through a major update and overhaul with large transformations happening in Future World.

Future World

Awesome Planet

This beautiful 10-minute show uses stunning visuals and in-theater effects such as wind and water to tell the story of planet Earth and why we must work to protect it.

Walt Disney Imagineering Presents The Epcot Experience

With Epcot undergoing a multi-year transformation, this pavilion allows you to take a peek into the future of the theme park.

Inside using screens and projections onto a 3D model you can discover the upcoming changes to the park.

These include the transformation of the park's icon - *Spaceship Earth*, a new Moana water walkthrough attraction, a Guardians of the Galaxy roller coaster with a backward launch, a new interactive Let's Play pavilion, the new *HarmonioUS* nighttime show, *Remy's Ratatouille Adventure*, and a new Mary Poppins attraction in the UK pavilion.

The full presentation takes about 12 minutes but you can walk in and out as you wish.

Test Track

A fun family thrill ride that takes you into the world of Chevrolet. In the queue line you design your own vehicle on a touchscreen, which is then virtually tested against other riders' vehicles throughout the ride.

The ride itself is a fun exploration of how different factors can influence a car and its capability, efficiency, responsiveness, and power.

This attraction is great fun but it is intense. It is the fastest ride at Walt Disney

 Yes Yes 40" 5 mins 60 to 120 mins

World and reaches speeds exceeding 60mph.

A Single Rider line is available.

Turtle Talk with Crush

This interactive show gets adults and kids alike to speak to Finding Nemo's Crush and ask him questions about the turtle world; meanwhile Crush has some questions for you about the human world.

 Yes No None 12 mins Less than 20 mins

It is a whole lot of fun if you are willing to get involved. You might even learn to speak whale!

Characters from "Finding Dory" also make appearances.

The Seas with Nemo and Friends

A slow-moving clamshell ride past one of the biggest aquariums in the world.

Stare in to take a look at the fish, and look out for characters from Pixar's Finding Nemo woven into the ride storyline mixed in

 Yes No None 4 mins Less than 20 mins

the same tanks as real fish.

After riding, enjoy Seabase - a 5.7-million-liter aquarium with interactive exhibitions, tutorials and glass panes to

see straight into the water and observe its inhabitants, as well as a Finding Dory's Friends scavenger hunt (free).

Living with the Land

A slow cruise with narration through greenhouses, fish farms and more.

Learn about the land, how humans use it and all it provides. Witness plant-growing technology techniques such as

Yes No None 14 mins Less than 30 mins

hydroponics - where plants are grown in water without soil.

A "Behind the Seeds" paid walking tour is also available

from the counter by *Soarin' Around the World*.

Look out for the added decorations around the Holiday period.

Mission: SPACE

Soar into space as you are put into an astronaut's shoes at Epcot.

Disney offers two versions of the ride. The "less intense" green version is still reasonably intense as simulators go. The "more intense" orange version spins rapidly to push and pull you from your seat for a more intense experience. This creates the feeling of zero gravity but is more likely to induce nausea.

 Yes No 40" ⌄ 4 mins ⧗ 30 to 45 mins

We suggest not eating before riding this attraction, or at least allow a few hours to digest your food, as this ride is known for inducing motion sickness.

The post-ride area is the *Advanced Training Lab*. This is a digital indoor play area (including chargers in the seats).

Journey into Imagination with Figment

This is perhaps the strangest attraction in all of Walt Disney World.

Your friend Figment (a purple dragon) wants to test out all five of your senses in this unusual slow-moving ride. It is a bizarre

Yes No None ⌄ 8 mins ⧗ Less than 10 mins

experience that is worth doing at least once.

The post-ride area is called ImageWorks, and is a variety of fun interactive games –

mostly to do with music.

The post-ride area can also be entered via the shop if you do not wish to ride the attraction.

Soarin' Around the World

One of Epcot's most popular attractions, *Soarin'* gives you the chance to experience flying and hang gliding over places around the world.

It is a truly immersive experience with smells and slow movement to match a

Yes No 40" ⌄ 5 mins ⧗ 60 to 90 mins

giant on-screen video, creating an incredibly realistic sensation of flight.

If you are scared of heights this ride is most definitely

not for you.

This is one of the best attractions in the park - the concept is simple but the execution is excellent.

Dining

Coral Reef Restaurant - Table Service, DDP accepted, entrées are $24-$40.
Garden Grill Restaurant- Table Service, No DDP, family-style with characters, breakfast is $27 for kids and $42 for adults, lunch & dinner is $36 for kids and $55 for adults.
Space 220 (Opening 2020) - Table Service. American cuisine with a view from space.
Sunshine Seasons - Snacks and Quick Service, DDP accepted, entrées are $9-$14.
Taste Track Burgers and Fries - Snacks and Quick Service, DDP accepted, prices vary seasonally.

World Showcase

The World Showcase is the second half of Epcot. Split into eleven countries located around a central lagoon, the World Showcase is your opportunity to explore different corners of the world, all just a stroll away from each other.

Explore World Showcase's pavilions and move from Canada to the UK in just a few steps, or travel to China and discover new cultures. Shop, dine, experience attractions, and speak to real representatives from the countries.

Note: With the exception of some food stands and dining locations, World Showcase and its attractions open at 11:00am, and not at 9:00am with Future World. The exceptions are the Norway and Mexico pavilions that open at 9:00am.

If you are staying at the hotels in the Epcot area or arriving on Disney's Skyliner, you may use the park's International Gateway entrance from park opening, and walk from World Showcase to Future World.

World Showcase Activities:
• **Disney Phineas and Ferb: Agent P's World Showcase Adventure** - Join Phineas and Ferb by becoming a special agent and exploring the countries' pavilions while completing missions on a specially designed phone. This is great for entertaining kids who might otherwise find the World Showcase area a bit boring.
• **Kidcot Fun Stops** - Designed for the youngest members of your party, each country around the World Showcase features these "fun stops" with a variety of activities for children to take part in as they make their way around the World Showcase.

Mexico

Gran Fiesta Tour Starring The Three Caballeros

A slow-moving boat ride through classic Mexican landscapes. While you are admiring the scenery, José Carioca and Panchito (two of the Three Cabelleros) are on the lookout for Donald Duck.

This is a gentle adventure that rarely has a wait. We recommend this cruise if you fancy a relaxing ride that is family-friendly - plus there is some fun lively music. It is a bit like *"it's a small world"* but just for Mexico.

🎟 Yes   📷 No   None   ⊘ 8 mins   ⧗ Less than 10 mins

Mexico Folk Art Gallery

This gallery features temporary exhibitions about Mexico and its culture.

Dining

Choza de Margarita - Bar, No DDP, drinks are $6-$15.50, small dishes are $4.50-$15
La Cava del Tequila - Bar, No DDP, drinks are $14-$21
La Cantina de San Angel - Quick Service, DDP accepted, entrées are $9.50-$14.50.
La Hacienda de San Angel - Table Service, DDP accepted, dinner only, entrées are $21-$36
San Angel Inn Restaurante - Table Service, DDP accepted, entrées are $18-$38

Norway
Frozen Ever After

This is an incredible adventure fit for the entire family. Guests are transported to the 'Winter in Summer Celebration', visit Elsa's Ice Palace and the North Mountain, along with other locations, before returning to the Bay of Arendelle.

This is an absolute must-do attraction. Minimize waits by getting here when the park opens, or reserve Fastpass+ well in advance.

FP Yes | 📷 Yes | None | ✓ 5 mins | ⧗ 90 to 150 mins

Stave Church Gallery

This gallery showcases Norwegian artifacts. Many of these details inspired the writers behind the hit Disney movie 'Frozen'. Exhibitions change periodically.

Royal Sommerhus

A well-themed and fun meet-and-greet with the Frozen sisters, Anna and Elsa. There is no Fastpass+ for this attraction, so expect to wait 20-45 minutes to meet the Frozen sisters.

Dining
Akershus Royal Banquet Hall - Buffet with Characters, DDP accepted, breakfast is $53 per adult and $34 per child, lunch & dinner is $63 per adult and $41 for kids.
Kringla Bakeri Og Kafe - Snacks and Quick Service, DDP accepted, entrées are $8-$10

China
Wondrous China (Opening 2020)

'Wondrous China' is a 360-degree movie inspiring you to visit this fascinating country. Along the journey, you can expect to see landmarks such as The Great Wall of China. This show is standing room only.

House of the Whispering Willows

This walk-through attraction features temporary exhibitions about China. At the time of writing, the exhibition is about Disney's newest resort, Shanghai Disneyland.

Dining
Joy of Tea - Snacks, DDP accepted, serves drinks, desserts and snacks, snacks are $4-$11
Lotus Blossom Café - Quick Service, DDP accepted, entrées are $10-$11
Nine Dragons Restaurant - Table Service, DDP accepted, entrées are $16-$25 at lunch and $16-$34 at dinner

---

Germany

Dining
Biergarten Restaurant - Buffet, DDP accepted, adult meals are $46 and children's are $29 at lunch and dinner
Sommerfest - Snacks and Quick Service, DDP accepted, sausages are $10.

The Germany pavilion only has a small outdoor area but it contains the huge Biergarten restaurant. There are stores here, but there are no attractions.

Italy

Dining
Gelati - Snacks, No DDP, ice creams are $7-$11.
Tutto Gusto Wine Cellar - Bar, No DDP, small dishes: $12-$26, entrees are $16-$32.
Tutto Italia Ristorante - Table Service, DDP accepted, entrées are $19-$36 at lunch & dinner.
Via Napoli Ristorante e Pizzeria - Table Service, DDP accepted, individual pizzas start at $23, and large family-size pizzas go for up to $49. Other entrees are $23-$36.

Enjoy the photo opportunities, dine, and shop. There are no attractions here.

Japan

The Japan pavilion is one of our favorites. It is serene, filled with beautiful photo opportunities, and you really do feel transported away from a busy theme park. Part of the reason for this is that there is no major attraction here.

Instead the majority of the pavilion is a huge shop that sells everything Japanese, from food to lampshades, and pearls to comic books.

The **Bijutsu-kan Gallery** features exhibits on Japanese history, which change regularly.

Dining
Kabuki Café - Snacks, No DDP, snacks and sushi are $5-$9.
Katsura Grill - Quick Service, DDP accepted, entrées are $9-$14.
Takumi-Tei - Signature Table Service, No DDP, entrees are $40-$120. A 9-course tasting menu is $180. Dinner only.
Teppan Edo - Table Service, DDP accepted, entrées are $24-$37.
Tokyo Dining - Table Service, DDP accepted, entrées are $21-$36.

The American Adventure

The American Adventure

Before watching this show, explore the inside of the pavilion building for paintings and quotes from historical American figures.

Get to the building well before showtime to enjoy the "Voices of Liberty" a cappella choir who sings patriotic songs, as well as Disney classics.

The show retells the U.S.A.'s history. It is educational and well-paced, but won't thrill.

 Yes No None 28 mins At set times

American Heritage Gallery

This gallery features temporary exhibits covering American history.

Dining

Fife & Drum Tavern - Snacks, DDP accepted, drinks are $4-$14, snacks are $5-$13.
Regal Eagle Smokehouse Inn - Quick Service, DDP accepted, entrées are $11.50-$19

Morocco

The Morocco pavilion is absolutely stunning and immediately stands out as one of the most authentic-looking pavilions. From the small passageways to the marketplace area with street sellers, it all feels very real.

Gallery of Arts and History

This gallery features temporary exhibits covering Moroccan history.

Dining

Restaurant Marrakesh - Table Service, DDP accepted, entrées are $22-$36, or $55 for a 3-course set meal
Spice Road Table - Table Service, DDP accepted, small plates are $9-$13, entrées: $25-$35
Tangierine Café - Quick Service, DDP accepted, entrées are $11-$17

Canada

Canada Far and Wide

Explore the wonder of the breadth of this beautiful country from the beautiful

Yes No None 13 mins Until next show

mountains to the dynamic cities. This show is standing room only as it is presented in 360-degree circle-vision.

Dining

Le Cellier Steakhouse - Table Service, DDP accepted – 2 Table Service credits, entrées: $34-$57

France

Remy's Ratatouille Adventure (Opening Summer 2020)

Due to open in summer 2020, *Ratatouille* is a trackless dark ride for the whole family. Here you board a 'ratmobile' and travel through Paris' streets, rooftops and kitchens in a 4D immersive ride featuring giant video screens, scents, water effects, and much more.

When it opens, this ride will be the newest in the park and therefore it will get the longest waits - expect waits of over two hours pretty much daily.

The ride will offer Fastpass+ and it *may* also have a Single Rider line if it follows Disneyland Paris (this is a clone of a ride there).

Impressions de France / Beauty and the Beast Sing-Along

This theater showcases two shows - currently this is *Impressions* until 7pm, and *Beauty and the Beast* after.

Explore France through a cinematic video on five screens spanning 220 degrees with well-known landmarks, and hidden gems in *Impressions de France*.

Alternatively, sing along to *Beauty and the Beast* songs.

No | No | None | 14 mins | Until next show

Dining

Chefs de France - Table Service, DDP accepted, entrées are $22-$37
Monsieur Paul - Signature Table Service Restaurant (2 credits required), DDP accepted, dinner only, entrées are $41-$47. There is also 3-course set menus at $89 and $119.
La Creperie de Paris - Table Service and Quick Service. Opens in 2020.
L'Artisan des Glaces - Snacks, No DDP, ice creams are $5-$12
Les Halles Boulangerie & Patisserie - Snacks, DDP accepted, items are $3-$11.

United Kingdom

Themed to a quaint English town, there is always a lot going on here, from the pub's atmosphere to the meet-and-greets to stage performances. There are, of course, many shops to explore.

There are no attractions at the UK pavilion.

Dining

Rose & Crown Pub & Dining Room - Table Service, DDP accepted, entrées are $21-$27
Yorkshire County Fish Shop - Quick Service, DDP accepted, meals are $11.50
UK Beer Cart - Drinks location, No DDP, alcoholic beverages are $10-$11

More about the World Showcase

World Showcase Transportation - The full walk around the World Showcase Lagoon (without exploring any of the countries) is 1.2 miles, but if you want to get across from one side to another quickly, catch one of the boats. Boats depart from the Future World side of the lagoon and go across to the Germany and Morocco pavilions.

Epcot's main entrance is by Spaceship Earth leading to Future World, but the park also has a "back" World Showcase entrance leading to the World Showcase located by the UK and French pavilions. It is most often used by those staying at the Boardwalk, Yacht and Beach Club, and Swan and Dolphin resorts, although anyone may use it. Boats to Disney's Hollywood Studios are here too. Guests arriving by Disney's Skyliner enter here.

Epcot Live Entertainment

JAMMitors (Future World) – Janitors use their tools to make music.

Mariachi Cobre (Mexican pavilion) – A Mexican folk band.

Sahara Beat (Moroccan pavilion) – Dance and sing to the rhythms of Morocco.

Jeweled Dragon Acrobats (Chinese pavilion) – This acrobatic troupe performs stunts.

Sergio (Italian pavilion) – A football juggler.

Voices of Liberty (American Adventure pavilion) – Incredible voices, and songs from throughout U.S. history, as well as Disney songs.

Matsuriza (Japanese pavilion) – Traditional Taiko drumming.

Serveur Amusant (French pavilion) – French acrobats dazzle with incredible skills.

Rose & Crown Pub Musician (UK pavilion) – Live music every evening.

Bodh'aktan (Canadian Pavilion) – Music that combines Celtic, Trad-Quebecois, Polka, Punk, Irish Folk, Breton and

Maritime.

Groovin' Alps (German Pavilion) – A high-energy German percussion band who brings the sounds of the mountains to Epcot with folk tunes played on items found on a farm.

Epcot Nighttime Spectacular - HarmonioUS

2020 brings Epcot a new nighttime spectacular - HarmonioUS.

Disney says: "This new show will celebrate how Disney music inspires people around the world, and will feature massive floating set pieces, custom-built LED panels, choreographed moving fountains, lights, pyrotechnics and lasers."

Disney's Hollywood Studios

Disney's Hollywood Studios was the third theme park built at Walt Disney World - it opened in 1989. The park is themed around Hollywood of the 1930s and 1940s. It hosted over 11.2 million guests in 2018, making it the ninth most visited theme park in the world, but the least visited park at Walt Disney World.

Park Entertainment

Citizens of Hollywood (Hollywood Boulevard) – Meet characters from Hollywood who present fun-filled shows during the day.

Fireworks – This park hosts seasonal nightly firework and projection shows most of the year.

Fantasmic – Fantasmic is Disney's Hollywood Studios' nighttime spectacular. The show combines character performances, water screen projections, fireworks, lasers, pyrotechnics and more. It should not be missed and appeals to all ages.

Arrive early to get the best seats in the 11,000-seat outdoor arena. If there are two performances on the same night, crowds will be smaller at the second one.

The Fastpass+ seating area takes up about half of the stadium-style seating, so be sure to arrive early, even with a Fastpass+ reservation, as there is no guarantee of a great view. Certain dining packages entitle you to reserved seating.

At off-peak times, *Fantasmic* only runs on select nights.

Hollywood Boulevard

Mickey & Minnie's Runaway Railway

Mickey & Minnie's Runaway Railway is the newest attraction at Disney's Hollywood Studios, having opened in March 2020.

The fun begins when you see the premiere of a new cartoon short with Mickey and Minnie getting ready for a picnic. As they head out, they drive alongside a train and see that the engineer is Goofy. Then, one magical moment lets you step into the movie and on Goofy's train for a wacky, wild ride.

Mickey & Minnie's Runaway Railway puts you inside the

FP+ Yes | 📷 No | No | ✓ 5 mins | ⏳ 60 to 90 mins

wacky and unpredictable world of a Mickey Mouse Cartoon Short where you're the star and anything can happen. It's a fun family-friendly ride.

Dining
The Hollywood Brown Derby - Table Service, DDP accepted, entrées are $18-$49. Lounge drinks are $14-$17. Small plates are $11-$20.
The Trolley Car Café - Starbucks location serving drinks and snacks, DDP accepted, drinks and snacks are $4-$6 each.

Sunset Boulevard

Sunset Boulevard contains many of the parks star attractions.

The Twilight Zone: Tower of Terror

The Tower of Terror transports you to another dimension dropping you 199 feet straight down.

The atmosphere is truly immersive and contains some of the best theming at Walt Disney World. The on-ride effects before the actual drops are great, and it really does feel like your elevator is out of control. The drops are fun but scary. The adrenaline is incredible, and it is definitely worth the visit.

Motors pull the elevator

 Yes Yes | 40" 7 mins 20 to 60 mins

down faster than gravity, creating a weightless feeling.

The ride has different drops each time.

Rock 'n' Roller Coaster: Starring Aerosmith

Rock 'n' Roller Coaster is a high-speed indoor roller coaster. Hop aboard a Limo and take a high-speed ride through the Hollywood hills. You will go through 4.5Gs and reach speeds of 60mph in 3 seconds.

Yes | Yes | 48" | 2 mins | 40 to 85 mins

Each Limo is equipped with speakers around your body for ultimate enjoyment. There are inversions and loops. If you are not a roller

coaster fan, then this ride is not for you.

A Single Rider line is available.

Lightning McQueen's Racing Academy

See a full-size Lightning McQueen show you his latest racing simulator in this fun 12-minute show. It is a good place to take a break with minimal waits, and great fun for Cars fans.

Beauty and the Beast - Live on Stage

Step into the world of Belle and Gaston for a whirlwind version of the Disney classic 'Beauty and the Beast'. This show is just like stepping into a Broadway performance with fantastic sets, costumes, and props. It is well worth a viewing. The theater is outdoors but covered.

Dining

Anaheim Produce - Snacks, No DDP, pretzels and churros are $6-$7. Serves drinks.
Catalina Eddie's - Quick Service, DDP accepted, entrées (pizza and salads) are $8-$11
Fairfax Fare - Quick Service, DDP accepted, entrées are $8-$13.50
Hollywood Scoops - Snacks, No DDP, ice creams are $5.50-$7
Rosie's All-American Café - Quick Service, DDP accepted, entrées $10-$13.50
Sunshine Day Bar - Quick Service, DDP accepted, drinks are $4-$14

Animation Courtyard

A mixture of shows and walkthroughs await you in this area of the park.

Walt Disney Presents

This walkthrough exhibit details the fascinating life of Walt Disney, from his humble beginnings to his vision for the Walt Disney World Resort years later.

As you move along the timeline you can read the information, watch videos, and see models of the original Disneyland.

You can even see the newest additions to Disney theme parks around the world. It is a fascinating insight for aspiring Imagineers.

At the end of the exhibition you can either exit or you can watch an 18-minute

No   No   None   10-30 mins   None

short movie retelling Walt Disney's life story - all narrated by the man himself.

The theater is often used to show extended movie

previews for upcoming Disney and Pixar productions. If this is the case during your visit, the preview will replace the movie about Walt Disney.

Voyage of The Little Mermaid

This show is a mixture of live actors, puppets, and light, laser and rain effects

 Yes   No   None   15 mins   At set times

retelling the story of The Little Mermaid. **Warning**: The large Ursula puppet used during the show may scare some younger children.

Disney Junior Dance Party!

With catchy songs, puppets and a toddler-friendly environment, Disney Junior Dance Party is designed for the younger members of the family. This live show experience takes its inspiration from popular Disney Junior shows on TV, including "Mickey and the Roadster Racers," "Doc McStuffins," "The Lion Guard" and "Vampirina."

Star Wars Launch Bay

This is a walkthrough exhibit featuring meet-and-greets with Star Wars characters, props from the movies and games to play. It is a haven for Star Wars fans.

Echo Lake

Star Tours - The Adventures Continue

Enter an intergalactic spaceport with StarSpeeders, an alien air traffic control station, and robots hard at work to make your journey into space unforgettable.

Then, board your vehicle for a tour of one of many planets — each time, the ride is slightly different, with over 50 different scene combinations!

Yes | No | 40" | 5 mins | 15 to 45mins

If you are prone to motion sickness *Star Tours* should be avoided as this is a motion simulator. If you want a milder ride, ask for the front row as the movements here are less jarring.

Jedi Training - Trials of the Temple

For the younger adventurers, this is the chance to get up on stage and yield a lightsaber and battle the dark side.

No | No | None | 15 mins | At set times

Unfortunately for adults, only children can participate in the experience and take part in the show.

For those not participating, the show is still entertaining to watch.

Jedi Training takes place to the left of *Star Tours: The Adventures Continue*.

Indiana Jones Epic Stunt Spectacular

See Indi and his friends take on some death-defying stunts. Get ready for set

Yes | No | None | 30 mins | At set times

changes, audience interaction, and an explosive finale. A definite must-watch for action fans.

For the First Time in Forever: A "Frozen" Celebration

Watch a retelling of the "Frozen" story with the historians of Arendelle. As

 Yes | No | None | 25 mins | At set times

the story evolves, the show becomes a sing-a-long every time a song comes on.

Dining
50's Prime Time Café - Table Service, DDP accepted, entrées are $17-$28
Backlot Express - Snacks and Quick Service, DDP accepted, entrées are $9-$14
Dockside Diner - Quick Service, DDP accepted, entrées are $11-$13
Epic Eats - Snacks, no DDP, desserts are $5.50-$8.50, drinks are $3.50-$14
Hollywood & Vine - Buffet Service, DDP accepted, breakfast is $42 per adult & $27 per child, lunch is $55 for adults & $36.
Tune-In Lounge - Bar, No DDP, drinks are $8 and upwards.

Commissary Lane & Grand Av.

For simplicity, we have combined these two park areas.

Muppet Vision 3D

Muppets fans, don't miss this 3D experience with in-theater special effects and

 Yes No None 30 mins Less than 15 mins

live action. The show time listed includes the pre-show.

Dining

ABC Commissary - Quick Service and Snacks, DDP accepted, entrées are $10-$18
Baseline Tap House - Lounge, No DDP, small plates $6-$11, also serves drinks
Sci-Fi Dine-In Theater Restaurant - Table Service, DDP accepted, entrées are $17-$33
Mama Melrose's Ristorante Italiano - Table Service, DDP accepted, entrées are $19-$33
Pizzerizzo - Quick Service, DDP accepted, entrées are $10-$11. Open seasonally.

Toy Story Land

Shrink down to the size of a toy to explore this world with Woody and his pals.

Toy Story Midway Mania

One of Walt Disney's most popular attractions, *Toy Story Midway Mania* is a virtual shooting experience where each rider uses a blaster to shoot at screens with Toy Story

 Yes No None 5 mins 45 to 75 mins

characters. In some scenes you will shoot plates, in others balloons, to get the most points.

It is great family fun but with an urge to win, you may find your arm aches after riding.

Slinky Dog Dash

Slinky Dog invites you aboard his family-friendly coaster. Get great views as you whiz across Toy Story Land on the Mega Coaster

 Yes Yes 38" 1 min 30 secs 60 to 90 mins

Play Kit that Andy's assembled. This is a good

starter coaster for kids - we suggest using FastPass+.

Alien Swirling Saucers

Hop inside a flying saucer powered by the Green Aliens from the Toy Story movies. You will spin on a wild ride into space as you whip around each corner.

 Yes No 32" 1 min 30 secs 40 to 60 mins

This attraction is very similar to the teacups at Magic Kingdom but with bigger

forces as you change direction. Fun for (almost) the whole family.

Dining

Woody's Lunch Box - Quick Service, DDP accepted, entrées are $6-$9 at breakfast and $9-$13 at lunch and dinner.
Woody's Roundup BBQ - Table Service. Opening in 2020.

Star Wars: Galaxy's Edge

Star Wars: Rise of the Resistance

Rise of the Resistance may be Disney's most incredible ride ever - it is part-simulator, park-dark ride and part-show.

 No No | 40" | ✓ 18 mins | ⧖ Boarding Groups

At the time of writing, the ride does not offer either a standby line nor Fastpass+ reservations. To ride, you must use the MyDisneyExperience app to get a Boarding Group on the day of your visit - you can do this from the official park opening time inside the park. You will need to be very quick as boarding groups for the whole day disappear in seconds - those with the fastest-fingers get to ride, those who are too slow, miss out. Each person in your party should try on their phones to increase your chance of success.

Disney will then send a notification to app users when it is their turn to ride - you won't be given a time slot to return if you succeed in getting a boarding group.

We expect that when demand dies down, the ride will use the regular standby line and Fastpass+ system. The 18-minute ride time includes several pre-shows.

Millennium Falcon: Smugglers Run

Smugglers Run is an interactive simulator, which is a bit like an upgraded version of *Star Tours*.

 Yes No | 38" | ✓ 5 mins | ⧖ 30 to 60 mins

In the queue, each guest is assigned a role for their flight - either a pilot, gunner, or engineer. Then, when you board your 6-seater vehicle be sure to stay alert to hear what you'll need to do to steer your ship to safety. Unlike, a normal simulator, here your actions have consequences so if you crash the Millennium Falcon, you'll know!

A Single Rider line is available.

As well as an incredibly-detailed area with lots of shopping, dining, and the two main attractions above, you may enjoy the following experiences available at an extra charge:
- **Savi's Workshop - Handbuilt Lightsabers** - In this 20-minute experience, you get to build a lightsaber from scratch. These lightsabers are much-better quality items than the normal ones and are not really toys but display pieces; and they should be - this workshop costs $200, plus tax. Reservations are recommended.
- **Droid Depot** - You build either a BB-style or R-style remote-controlled droid. You choose your parts from a conveyor belt, build your droid and then activate it. The whole experience takes about 20 minutes. You are given a carry box for your droid but may not play with the droid on the ground inside the park. The droid will interact with the different areas of Galaxy's Edge through various beeps, lights and movements and will react when it sees other droids. The droid experience is $100 - to add a backpack is an additional $50.

Dining
Kat Saka's Kettle - Snacks. DDP accepted. Sells popcorn ($6.50), orb soda ($5.50) & water.
Ronto Roasters - Quick Service. DDP accepted. Serves oats ($7), wraps ($12.50) and snack samplers ($20). Also serves alcoholic ($13-$15) beverages, as well as hot and cold drinks.
Docking Bay 7 Food and Cargo - Quick Service. DDP accepted. Serves breakfast. Lunch and dinner entrees include pot roast, pork ribs and chicken salad ($14-$19).
Oga's Cantina - Bar/Lounge. No DDP. Serves non-alcoholic ($7-$13) and alcoholic drinks ($17-$45) including Blue Milk, plus snacks.
Milk Stand - Snack Kiosk. DDP accepted. Serves snacks and Blue and Green milk as a non-alcoholic ($8) or alcoholic drink ($14).

Disney's Animal Kingdom Park

Disney's Animal Kingdom Park is Walt Disney World's fourth and newest theme park. It opened on Earth Day (April 22) in 1998. Spanning 580 acres, it is the largest Disney park ever built. It is so big that you could fit all the other theme parks at Walt Disney World inside it and have room to spare.

Animal Kingdom is, in our opinion, the best themed of all the parks with remarkable attention to detail. The park does not, however, have very many attractions and can be "seen" in less than a day. This is the sixth most visited park in the world, with 13.7 million visitors in 2018.

The entrance area of the park is called **Oasis**. It is a forest-like setting that immerses you in winding pathways and a stunning atmosphere from the moment you step in. The **Oasis Exhibits** are home to exotic animals housed along tropical garden pathways. For those wanting to eat in this area, **Rainforest Café** is accessible from both inside and outside the park (Table Service, DDP accepted, entrées are $9-$16 at breakfast, and $17-$37 at lunch and dinner) .

Live Shows

Festival of the Lion King

Festival of The Lion King is our favorite show at Walt Disney World and a true celebration of the essence of The Lion King movies.

The show does not follow a movie storyline, but instead includes the best songs interpreted by professionals in an African-inspired theme. This is a definite must-do. This show is presented in the Africa area of the park.

 Yes No ┃ None ⊙ 30 mins ⧖ At set times

Finding Nemo: The Musical

This Broadway-style show has convinced us that Finding Nemo should have been a musical all along!

The show has great sets,

Yes No ┃ None ⊙ 40 mins ⧖ At set times

costumes and actors. Take the time to see this family-friendly production.

This show is located in the Dinoland USA area of the park.

Rivers of Light: We are One - Nighttime Spectacular

This nighttime spectacular features live music, floating lanterns, water screens and swirling animal imagery bringing a show to Discovery River that delights guests

 Yes No ┃ None ⊙ 16 mins ⧖ At set times

and truly caps off their day.

Dedicated viewing and

seating areas are available in Asia and Dinoland USA.

Discovery Island

This is the hub area of the park that holds the astounding Tree of Life, and leads to all the other lands of the park.

Tree of Life

Discover over 320 animals carved into this 145-foot tall tree, as you walk around it. The attention to detail is amazing – a true masterpiece.

At the Discovery Island trails, you can find otters, lemurs, flamingos, red kangaroos, storks, tortoises and more on these self-guided walks.

After sunset, see the tree of life's "awakenings" throughout the evening.

It's Tough to be a Bug

The meanest and nastiest 4D show we have ever experienced. Be prepared to see how humans treat insects and then get a taste of your own medicine. Even when you think it is over, it is

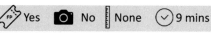

FP: Yes | Camera: No | None | 9 mins | Less than 20 mins

not! This attraction is likely to frighten adults, and terrify children. We do not recommend making

Fastpass+ reservations as the queues for this show are usually short.

Adventurers Outpost Meet and Greet

Get a photo with Mickey and Minnie in their Safari gear at this location. This is often

FP: Yes | Camera: No | None | 1-2 mins | Less than 30 mins

one of the least crowded meet and greets featuring Mickey across all four parks.

Winged Encounters – The Kingdom Takes Flight

This show takes place in front of the Tree of Life. It features different types of macaw and gives guests a chance to see them up close.

Dining

Creature Comforts - Starbucks, DDP accepted, drinks and snacks are $3-$6
Eight Spoon Café - Snacks, no DDP, individual snacks are $3-$7.
Flame Tree Barbecue - Snacks and Quick Service, DDP accepted, entrées are $11-$19
Isle of Java - Snacks, no DDP, pastries, pretzels and biscuits are $4-$7.
Nomad Lounge - Bar and lounge, No DDP, small plates are $9 to $18, drinks vary in price.
Pizzafari - Quick Service, DDP accepted, pizzas, salads and flatbreads are $10-$13.50
Tiffins - Signature Table Service, DDP accepted (2 Table Service credits), entrées are $30-$65.

DinoLand U.S.A.

Themed to a traveling carnival, DinoLand has several attractions listed below. As well as these, there are also the Fossil Fun Games (carnival-style games – extra charge to play) and The Boneyard (a play area) to explore.

DINOSAUR

This is an intense, loud and turbulent journey through the past as you venture in search of an iguanodon dinosaur. However, things may not go quite to plan.

This ride is a great thrill with an incredible ride vehicle, great storytelling, and an immersive storyline.

It is a fun blast into the past but will likely scare younger visitors due to the darkness and the loud sound effects throughout the attraction.

Yes · Yes · 40" · 3 mins · 20 to 45 mins

TriceraTop Spin

This is a spinning ride just like *Dumbo* at the Magic Kingdom, but themed to dinosaurs. It is fun, but nothing revolutionary, and

No · No · None · 1 min 30 secs · Less than 15 mins

usually has short queues. You can control your dinosaur's height with a lever. Great for younger kids.

Primeval Whirl

Primeval Whirl spins you round and round back in time to the prehistoric ages. The ride has some tight corners, short drops and lots of spinning. This may be too

Yes · No · 48" · 1 min 30 secs · 20 to 60 mins

intense for a first roller coaster but it is a good mid-range coaster.

This ride operates seasonally and may not be open during your visit.

Dining

Dino-Bite Snacks - Snacks, No DDP, serves ice creams at $5.50-$8
Dino Diner - Snacks, No DDP, serves chip pies and hot/corn dogs at $8.50-$11
Restaurantosaurus - Quick Service, DDP accepted, entrées are $10-$17
Trilo-Bites - Snacks, No DDP, sells ice creams and shakes for $5-$6, and drinks

Africa

Travel to the African continent into a land filled with character and spice.

Kilimanjaro Safaris

Traverse the world's largest man-made savannah, spanning 110 acres on-board Kilimanjaro Safaris.

Join your guide for a ride on a safari-style truck and get closer to the animals than you ever thought possible at a theme park.

Make sure you bring your camera as you may just get to see hippos, giraffes, monkeys, zebras, lions, and more on this unpredictable adventure. It really is different every single time.

The queue line for this attraction is tedious, so we

| FP Yes | 📷 No | None | ⌄ 20 mins | ⏳ 30 to 60 mins |

recommend you make a FastPass+ reservation if possible.

Top Tip: The animals are

most active in the morning, before it gets too hot, so try to get to this attraction early.

Gorilla Falls Exploration Trail

See gorillas, monkey, meerkats, birds and more in this self-guided walkthrough attraction. This is a relaxing change from the long waits of many of the major attractions at this park. Here you can take the animals in at your own pace.

Wildlife Express Train

Ride the Wildlife Express Train for a scenic trip from Harambe, Africa to Rafiki's Planet Watch.

Dining

Dawa Bar - Bar, No DDP, drinks are $9-$14

Harambe Fruit Market - Snacks, DDP accepted, fruit is $2-$6

Harambe Market - Quick Service, DDP accepted, entrées are $10-$13.50

Kusafiri Coffee Shop & Bakery - Snacks and Quick service, No DDP, curries are $10.50-$11.50

Tamu Tamu Refreshments - Drinks and Desserts, No DDP, ice creams are $6-$7 and alcoholic drinks are $9-$11.

Tusker House Restaurant - Buffet, DDP accepted, the character breakfast is $42 per adult and $27 per child. The non-character lunch and dinner buffet is $55 per adult, and $36 per child.

Rafiki's Planet Watch

To get to Rafiki's Planet Watch you will need to catch the Wildlife Express Train from the Africa area of the park.

Animal Exhibits

• **Habitat Habit!** - Learn about how to protect endangered cotton-top tamarins in their natural homes. Guests also learn how to create animal habitats in their own homes.

• **Conservation Station** - See the conservation efforts undertaken by The Walt Disney Company and take a behind the scenes look at how the animals are taken care of at Disney's Animal Kingdom, including a look at an examination room.

• **Affection Section** - This is essentially a petting zoo with domesticated animals. Cast Members may be present to tell you facts about the animals here.

It All Started with a Mouse

 No No None 20 mins ⧗ At set times

Conservation Station's "animal ambassadors" including sheep, parrots, porcupines, birds of prey and Kunekune pigs help tell stories and make appearances in, around, and even above the audience in this show.

Cast Members share natural history fun facts, conservation messages and inspiring calls-to-action.

After the show, meet some of the stars of the show and capture once-in-a-lifetime memories with plenty of photographs.

Asia

Expedition Everest - Legend of the Forbidden Mountain

Expedition Everest is an incredible ride through the Forbidden Mountain where you might just get to see The Yeti in his natural habitat! The queue line is incredible - you even pass through a yeti museum while waiting!

As well as the big drop outside the attraction, there are a few other surprises. The ride reaches speeds of 50mph (80km/h). Expedition Everest is great fun and very smooth - this is one of Disney's best-ever rides!

 Yes Yes 44" ⌄ 3 mins ⌛ 30 to 70 mins

Maharajah Jungle Trek

This self-guided walk has Komodo dragons, fruit bats, pythons, Bengal tigers, birds, deer, water buffalo and more. This is a must-visit for animal fans and we think it is the most exciting and interesting of the trails, although this will depend on which animals you prefer to see.

Kali River Rapids

This fun raft water ride takes you through the forest. Everyone gets at least a little bit wet - but one or two people will be soaked.

This attraction is particularly popular on hot summer

Yes No 38" ⌄ 4 mins ⌛ 45 to 75 mins

days. We recommend making a Fastpass+ reservation as the queue line is slow.

There are free lockers outside the ride entrance for storing belongings. There is also a storage area in the center of the raft.

UP! A Great Bird Adventure

A bird show with a fun storyline, a range of birds and some impressive tricks, as well as Doug and Russell from the hit-movie 'Up!'.

The seating area is covered, providing shade and shelter,

but it is not air-conditioned. This 25-minute show plays several times daily in the Asia area of the park.

Dining

Anandapur Ice Cream Truck - Snacks, no DDP, ice creams are $5-$5.50.
Drinkwallah - Snacks and drinks, drinks are $3.50-$5.50, chips and nut snacks are $3-$6.
Mr. Kamal's - Snacks, DDP accepted, dumplings, hummus and fries are $5-$6 each.
Thirsty River Bar and Trek Snacks - Bar and Snacks, No DDP, snacks are $3-$7
Warung Outpost - Snacks, No DDP, sells pretzels ($7), chips ($3) and drinks incl. alcohol
Yak & Yeti Local Food Cafes - Quick Service, DDP accepted, entrées are $9-$12 at breakfast and $12-$15 at lunch and dinner
Yak & Yeti Quality Beverages Lounge - Bar, No DDP, entrées are $12-$16 and drinks are $4-$11
Yak & Yeti Restaurant - Table Service, DDP accepted, small plates, entrées are $19-$32

Pandora: World of Avatar

Inspired by the highest-grossing film of all time, Pandora: World of Avatar is Animal Kingdom's newest area - it opened in Summer 2017.

AVATAR: Flight of Passage

Flight of Passage is Animal Kingdom's most popular attraction, and one of the most technologically advanced attractions Disney has ever created.

This motion simulator has you sitting on the back of a Banshee (flying creature) and then soaring around the world of Pandora - around mountains, water and scenery.

| FP Yes | No | 44" | 5 mins | 120 to 180 mins |

Through the 3D goggles, HD video and all kinds of clever sensory techniques, you are transported to another world - this is an immersive experience not to miss.

Guests who are scared of heights or simulated drops may wish to avoid this ride.

The ride vehicles are individual motorbike-style restraints and may not accommodate larger guests.

Expect long wait times all day - head here as soon as the park opens if you don't manage to get a Fastpass+ reservation. On the busiest of days, expect to see a wait of up to 4 hours.

Na'vi River Journey

Na'vi River Journey is Pandora's more family-friendly attraction. Here you sit on a riverboat and calmly pass the nighttime jungle scenery of Pandora.

You'll see creatures, bioluminescent plants and other forest life around you.

The most impressive part of the ride is when you see a shaman beating musical drums - this is an incredibly lifelike animatronic (pictured) that has to be seen to be believed. There are no moments that should frighten kids.

| FP Yes | No | None | 5 mins | 60 to 90 mins |

Dining
Pongo Pongu - Bar and Snacks, DDP accepted, snacks are $3-11 and drinks are $3.50-$13
Satu'li Canteen - Quick Service, DDP accepted, entrées are $12.50-$17

MyMagic+

MyMagic+ is Disney's vacation-planning tool made up of three main components: My Disney Experience, FastPass+ (see in next chapter), and MagicBands.

MyDisneyExperience

This is a website and a mobile app that allow you to:
• Get you all the information you need in one place; plan as much, or as little, as you want.
• Make dining, FastPass+ and other reservations in advance
• See your in-park photos, including ride photos
• Purchase Memory Maker to receive access to all photos and videos from your vacation
• Purchase park tickets
• See park maps
• See wait times for attractions and selected meet and greet experiences

MagicBands

Disney resort hotel guests are entitled to use an RFID-enabled MagicBand that ties together all the features of MyMagic+.

The MagicBand is worn on your wrist throughout your vacation. It allows you to check-in for Disney's Magical Express, open your Disney resort hotel room door, pay for food and merchandise, use Disney Dining Plans, make and use FastPass+ reservations, use Disney's Photopass service, have automatic on-ride photos, and enter the theme parks and water parks.

MagicBands are shipped 10 to 30 days before arrival to US addresses, or to the resort if your reservation is made within 10 days of arrival. International visitors receive their MagicBand at hotel check-in.

If you are not staying at a Disney resort hotel, you can purchase a MagicBand for $14.99 from Walt Disney World Resort stores,

although MagicBands do not do very much for non-Disney hotel guests except allow you to tap into the parks and attractions instead of using your park ticket, and linking photos and videos to PhotoPass and Memory Maker accounts.

MagicBands & special events:
Throughout the year, in-park events take place outside of regular park hours, and require a separate 'hard ticket' such as Magic Kingdom's Halloween and Christmas parties. You can seamlessly use your MagicBands during events.

You can link your separate 'hard ticket' admission ticket to your "My Disney Experience" account by entering the ticket number on the website or the app. If you bought the ticket on the Disney website, you may find that it is already automatically linked. This allows you to enter the park with a MagicBand instead of

using a paper ticket.

You will be given a physical 'event wristband' for special events at the park entrance if you enter after a certain time. Guests who enter the park before this time will need to present themselves at a designated location inside the park to pick up an event wristband. You must wear an event wristband during special events, as well as optionally wearing a MagicBand.

Fastpass+ is not available during hard ticketed events. Only stand-by queue lines are used. Touch to Pay, PhotoPass, and Memory Maker work as normal.

FastPass+

Walt Disney World offers a FREE time-saving system, called FastPass+.

How to Make FastPass+ Reservations

The steps are similar on the MyDisneyExperience (MDE) website, the app, or the in-park FastPass+ kiosks.

Sign in to MDE. Link your park tickets and hotels. At in-park kiosks, just touch your MagicBand.

• Select 'FastPass+'. Choose the date and theme park you want to make a FP+ reservation for.
• Select the people you are making FP+ reservations for.
• Select a time for your FP+ reservations.
   o At *Magic Kingdom*, choose any three experiences.
   o At *Epcot, Animal Kingdom* and *Disney's Hollywood Studios,* choose 1 attraction from Tier 1 and 2 attractions from Tier 2.

More information on these Tiers on page 91.
• You will see all available 1-hour FP+ reservation slots.
• You can make up to three advanced FP+ reservations per day for one theme park (but only one per ride).

When it is time to use your FP+ reservation, go to the attraction, tap your MagicBand or park ticket on the Mickey head by the FP+ entrance to enter the FP+ queue line which provides expedited attraction entry.

The FP+ reservation is for a specific booked time, except a 5-minute leeway before and 15 minutes after. If an attraction breaks down, the FP+ reservation is valid all day.

During your visit you can add and change FP+ reservations at in-park kiosks or with the MDE app.

If you arrive without FP+ reservations, you can make up to 3 FP+ reservations at the park using one of the FP+ kiosks or the MDE app.

When can I make FastPass+ Reservations?

Staying On-Site
If you are staying at a Walt Disney World Resort hotel, 60 days before your check-in date, you can make FastPass+ reservations for up to three experiences for each day of your vacation online via the MDE website or app.

If staying at a Disney hotel, you can make FastPass+ reservations for their whole stay (up to 14 days all at once).

Staying Off-Site
If you are not staying at a Disney hotel, you can make FastPass+ reservations up to 30 days in advance. You must have bought your tickets before your visit begins and linked these on MDE (you will need to register for a free account).

Off-site guests need to visit MDE daily 30 days before each day of their vacation.

More Details
You can make FastPass+ reservations starting at 7:00am Eastern Time either 30 or 60 days before your vacation. If you are not logged in at 7:00am EST, you will likely miss some of the most popular FastPass+ experiences.

Disney Club Level Extra FastPass+ - If you book Club Level at a Disney resort hotel, you can purchase an extra 3 FastPass+ reservations - for an additional $50 per person per day. These FastPass+ reservations can be made 90 days before your check-out date. This is not good value for money, in our opinion, but if you have very limited time, this may make sense. If that's not you, follow the tips in this chapter instead.

"Additional" same-day FP+ reservations

• **Once you have used all 3 of your advanced FastPass+ reservations, you can make additional in-park FP+ reservations** on the MDE app or at in-park kiosks. Don't make your FP+ reservations for late in the day, so you can take advantage of these "additional" same-day FP+ reservations.

• *Epcot, Animal Kingdom* and *Hollywood Studios* use a tiered system for your advanced reservations. After you have used all 3 initial FP+ reservations, you can "additional" same-day FP+ reservations for any attraction, regardless of its tier. The tier system does not apply to "additional reservations".

• **With the "additional" FP+ reservations,** you can choose any attraction at any park if it has a FP+ slot free – you do not have to be inside the park you want to use the FastPass+ in when making the reservation.

For example, if you spend the morning at Magic Kingdom Park using your pre-booked FastPass+ reservations and want to book a FastPass+ attraction at Epcot, you can do this while at Magic Kingdom.

• **You can only make one "additional" reservation at a time.** Once your "additional" FastPass+ reservation has been used, you can make another FastPass+ reservation. Repeat this as many times as you want.

How to get a 'Hard-to-Get' FastPass+ Res.?

Log into MDE's FastPass+ page at exactly 7:00am Eastern Time, either 30 days before your trip (for non-Disney hotel guests) or 60 days before (for Disney hotel guests). You must be logged in this early for the most popular FP+ experiences.

Even being logged in this far in advance, some FastPass+ reservations are very difficult to get – *Mickey & Minnie's Runaway Railway, Millennium Falcon: Smugglers Run, Frozen Ever After, Seven Dwarfs Mine Train, Slinky Dog* and *AVATAR: Flight of Passage* are some good examples.

If you cannot get a FastPass+ reservation by being early, there is a solution. This strategy works both with advance FastPass+ reservations and those made on the day.

Gaming the System
MyDisneyExperience searches for FastPass+ availability for all members in your party at the same time.

So, if you want to visit *Toy Story Mania* and there are 4 people in your party, the system will look for a time slot for 4 people to ride together. If it cannot find a slot for 4 people, it will say there is no availability.

However, if you look for a slot for only 2 or 3 people, you may find availability. You should look for a FP+ reservation for a lower number of people than are in your party first. Then, once you have confirmed that reservation, look for another reservation for the remaining party members.

With some luck, the reservation times will overlap and you can all ride together! If they do not overlap, take the FastPass+ reservations anyway and modify the times later - this is usually possible.

List of FastPass+ Experiences and Tiers

An asterisk (*) next to a ride name means it is a top pick for choosing as a FP+ reservation.

Magic Kingdom:
- Big Thunder Mtn Railroad
- Buzz Lightyear's Space Ranger Spin
- Dumbo the Flying Elephant
- Enchanted Tales with Belle
- Haunted Mansion
- "it's a small world"
- Jungle Cruise
- Mad Tea Party
- Meet Ariel at Ariel's Grotto
- Meet Cinderella
- Meet Rapunzel
- Meet Mickey Mouse
- Meet Tinker Bell
- Mickey's Philharmagic
- Monsters Inc. Laugh Floor
- Peter Pan's Flight*
- Pirates of the Caribbean
- Seven Dwarfs Mine Train*
- Space Mountain*
- Splash Mountain*
- The Barnstormer
- The Magic Carpets of Aladdin
- The Many Adventures of Winnie the Pooh
- Tomorrowland Speedway
- Under the Sea: Journey of the Little Mermaid

At Magic Kingdom, you can choose any combination of experiences. At Epcot, Animal Kingdom and Hollywood Studios you choose one attraction from Tier 1, and two from Tier 2.

Epcot:
Tier 1 (Choose one attraction):
- Frozen Ever After*
- HarmonioUS
- Remy's Ratatouille Adventure (expected)*
- Soarin'*
- Test Track*

Tier 2 (Choose two attractions):
- Disney & Pixar Short Film Festival
- Journey into Imagination with Figment
- Living with the Land
- Mission: SPACE
- The Seas with Nemo & Friends
- Turtle Talk with Crush

Disney's Hollywood Studios:
Tier 1 (Choose one attraction):
- Mickey & Minnie's Runaway Railway*
- Millennium Falcon: Smugglers Run*
- Slinky Dog Dash*

Tier 2 (Choose two attractions):
- Alien Swirling Saucers
- Beauty and the Beast - Live on Stage
- Disney Junior Dance Party!
- Fantasmic!
- For the First Time in Forever: A Frozen Sing-Along Celebration
- Indiana Jones Epic Stunt Spectacular!
- Muppet*Vision 3D
- Rock 'n' Roller Coaster
- Star Tours
- The Twilight Zone Tower of Terror
- Toy Story Midway Mania!*
- Voyage of the Little Mermaid

Disney's Animal Kingdom:
Tier 1 (Choose one attraction):
- Avatar Flight of Passage*
- Na'vi River Journey*

Tier 2 (Choose two attractions):
- Adventurers Outpost
- Dinosaur
- Expedition Everest*
- Festival of the Lion King
- Finding Nemo: The Musical
- It's Tough to be a Bug
- Kali River Rapids*
- Kilimanjaro Safaris
- Primeval Whirl
- Rivers of Light - We Go On
- Up! A Great Bird Adventure

Park Touring Strategies

This chapter is intended to help you tour the parks and reduce your time waiting in queue lines. It is not a complete touring plan but strategies of when to do certain attractions.

Before we begin...

You should be at the park at least 30 minutes before the official opening time of each park, with your park ticket in hand, to make the most of these touring strategies.

Top Tip 1: The theme parks regularly allow guests in up to 45 minutes before the published opening time, with select attractions open. Being at the park entrance early lets you take advantage

of this 'secret early entry'.

Top Tip 2: As long as you are in a queue line by the closing time of a theme park, you can experience the attraction, no matter how long the wait is. E.g. It is 9:59pm and the Magic Kingdom closes at 10:00pm and the wait time for *Buzz* is 25 minutes. Get in line now and you will still ride even though you will ride after

the official park closing time.

Top Tip 3: If you wish to ride one of the top attractions without a FastPass+ reservation, do not do this on a day with morning Extra Magic Hours (EMHs) as the parks are much busier than they would otherwise be. You should especially avoid these days if you don't have EMH access as the park is busy before you even enter.

Magic Kingdom

Big Thrills:
Make FastPass+ reservations for *Peter Pan's Flight, Seven Dwarfs Mine Train* and *Jungle Cruise*.

If you can't get an advanced FastPass+ reservation for *Seven Dwarfs Mine Train*, go there first and then follow the next step.

If you do have a *Seven Dwarfs Mine Train* reservation, the first thing you should do at park opening is to ride the three 'mountains' in this order: *Space Mountain, Big Thunder Mountain* and *Splash Mountain*. You can often do all of these within the first hour of park opening. Later in the day, these often have waits of two hours each.

After 9:30pm (assuming *Happily Ever After* is showing

at 10:00pm), most rides will have a line of 10 minutes or less – *Under the Sea, Buzz Lightyear* and *Winnie the Pooh* are three examples of rides which have waits of about 60 minutes most of the day but have no wait in the evening. The same also applies to *Peter Pan's Flight* which does not usually have a wait of more than 20 minutes this late at night (despite what may be posted as the wait time).

At shows such as *Carousel of Progress, Monsters Inc. Laugh Floor, Mickey's Philharmagic, Country Bear Jamboree* and *Enchanted Tiki Room*, you should never wait more than 15 minutes. If the wait time is longer, come back later.

Kids' Favorites:
Make your FastPass+ reservations for the *Seven*

Dwarfs Mine Train, Jungle Cruise and *Enchanted Tales with Belle*. Those who want to meet the princesses in *Fairytale Hall* should make this their most important Fastpass+ reservation (substituting *Jungle Cruise*). Check the height requirement for *Seven Dwarfs Mine Train*.

At park opening, ride *Peter Pan's Flight* first, followed by *The Barnstormer, Winnie the Pooh* and *Under the Sea*. You can usually do these four rides within the first 60 minutes of the park opening provided you keep up the pace. Work your way around Fantasyland.

The wait time for *"it's a small word"* rarely exceeds 25 minutes so you can do that at any point of the day; the same applies to all of the shows.

Epcot

Frozen Ever After is Epcot's second-newest ride and with the popularity of Frozen as strong as ever, this ride usually has the longest wait in the park along with *Ratatouille*. You should make a FastPass+ reservation for either of these attractions in advance - you will leave the other for the end of the day.

Test Track is the third most popular attraction in this park. Go here first as soon as the park opens.

Next, head over to *Soarin'*, and then ride *Mission: Space*. This will involve a lot of going back and forth but it is the best use of your time.

Once you have done these three rides, all the major long-lined rides are done - except *Frozen Ever After* and *Ratatouille*!

Alternatively, if you are happy splitting up your group, ride *Soarin'* first followed by *Test Track* in the

Single Rider line.

The Magic Eye Theater, The Seas with Nemo and Friends, Journey into Imagination with Figment and *Living with the Land* very rarely have waits of over 20 minutes, with most of these being walk-ons all day long.

If the wait is longer than this for any of these attractions, then return later in the day.

Disney's Hollywood Studios

Try and get a Boarding Group for *Star Wars: Rise of the Resistance* using the process described on page 80.

Assuming you have a FastPass+ reservation for *Slinky Dog* or *Mickey and Minnie's Runaway Railway*, at park opening, you should ride whichever one you don't have a Fastpass for. Then, ride *Toy Story Midway Mania*.

Avoid this park on a day when it has morning Extra Magic Hours if you are not staying at a Disney hotel.

After *Midway Mania*, ride *Rock 'n' Roller Coaster* and then *Tower of Terror*.

Most of the other attractions are shows – get there 20 minutes before they start for a good seat.

Voyage of the Little

Mermaid sometimes has waits of over 30 minutes. If this is the case, come back later. The show runs continuously throughout the day – you should not have to wait any longer than until the next show starts (every 20 minutes or so).

Star Tours' wait time fluctuates throughout the day, but you shouldn't wait for more than 20 minutes.

Disney's Animal Kingdom

Ideally you should have a FastPass+ reservation for *AVATAR: Flight of Passage*. If so, head for *Na'vi River Journey*. If not, head straight to *AVATAR: Flight of Passage* at park opening. Be at the park gates at least 1 hour before opening (not 30 minutes like the other parks). Then, follow this plan - save *Na'vi River Journey* for the very end of the day.

Expedition Everest should be next, followed by *Kilimanjaro Safaris* (the animals are most active in the morning!) and then *Kali River Rapids*.

On very hot days, waits for *Kali River Rapids* get long from 11:00am onwards. If this is a priority, make a FastPass+ reservation.

DINOSAUR's wait time fluctuates during the day but you shouldn't wait more than 20 minutes. If it is longer, come back later.

Primeval Whirl has one of the longest and most tedious queues in the park. Avoid the wait by making a FastPass+ reservation.

Everything else is a show; turn up 15 to 20 minutes before the start time.

Blizzard Beach Water Park
Disney Water Park Basics and Tips

• Mats, inner tubes, life jackets, changing room, showers, car parking and floatation devices are free.
• Seating and cabanas can be reserved for a charge.

• Entry into one water park is $69.03 for adults and $62.84 for children, incl tax.
• Lockers are $10 for a small locker and $15 for a large locker. Towel rentals are $2.

• Children of diaper age must wear tight rubber pants over their diapers, or swimming diapers.
• Swimsuits with metal are not allowed on slides.

Green Slope

Summit Plummet – 48” (1.22m) or taller to ride. This is the park's premier attraction. At 120-feet tall it is one of the tallest and fastest free-fall slides in the world with speeds of up to 60mph!

Teamboat Springs – The longest "family white-water raft ride" in the world at 1,400 feet (427 m) in length. Board a big blue raft with room for four to six people!

Slush Gusher – 48”(1.22m) or taller to ride. This body slide has you reaching speeds of up to 35 mph - you really get "air time".

Red Slope

Runoff Rapids – Several 600-foot inner tube slides – two are open-air and one is enclosed. You can't race as all the slides are different lengths. Access to this attraction is via stairs only.

Purple Slope

Downhill Double Dipper – 48” (1.22m) or taller to ride. A racing slide with a countdown and automated gates.

Snow Stormers – A mat slide where you lie on your stomach on a toboggan-style mat. There are 3 flumes; each is 350-feet long.

Toboggan Racers – 8 identical lanes, each 250-feet-long. Guests line up and wait for the signal, then push off, and race!

Ground Level

The Chairlift – A ride from Ground Level to the top of Mount Gushmore. Guests must be at least 32” tall to ride (or 48”/1.22m tall to ride alone).

Cross Country Creek – A 3000-foot-long lazy river around the park. The full loop takes 20 to 30 minutes.

Melt-Away Bay – A wave pool with small waves.

Tike's Peak – Kiddie versions of the big slides. Plus, a fountain play area. Guests must be 48” (1.22m) tall or shorter.

Ski Patrol Training Camp – Split into several areas: *Cool Runners* is an inner tube area, *Leisure Pool* has icebergs for kids to walk on, *Freezin' Pipe Springs* is a body slide and *Fahrenheit Drops* drops guests under five feet (1.52 m) tall into 8.5 feet (2.6 m)-deep water.

Dining
Avalunch - Snacks and Quick Service, DDP accepted, entrées are $10-$11
Cooling Hut - Sandwiches, snacks, desserts and drinks, DDP accepted, prices are $4-$11
Frostbite Freddy's Frozen Freshments - Snacks, No DDP, entrées & desserts are $4.50-$12
I.C. Expeditions - Snacks, No DDP, snacks are $4.50-$14
Lottawatta Lodge - Snacks and Quick Service, DDP accepted, entrées are $8.50-$11
Mini Donuts - Snacks, donuts and drinks, No DDP, donuts are $5-$10
Polar Pub - Bar, serves alcoholic and non-alcoholic drinks, No DDP, $3-$11
Warming Hut - Snacks and Quick Service sandwiches, DDP accepted, entrées are $9-$11

Typhoon Lagoon Water Park
Surfing School at Typhoon Lagoon

Typhoon Lagoon's wave pool is the perfect place to learn to surf. Several surf schools are offered. These run on selected dates early in the morning. Classes are of up to 13 people with 2 instructors, and $190 per person (including tax). Surfboards are provided. Due to the early start time, resort hotel transportation is not available, but hotel buses run by the time the class ends. Book up to 90 days in advance on 407-WDW-PLAY.

Attractions

Mount Mayday

Humunga Kowabunga – Guests must be 48" (1.22m) or taller to ride. Reach speeds of up to 39mph and slide down five stories on each of the three enclosed "speed slides".

Gangplank Falls – A family slide with inner tubes connected for 4 people.

Storm Slides – Three body slides that twist and turn leaving riders in a splash pool at the bottom.

Mayday Falls – A tube slide that creates the feeling of being in "rough rapids".

Keelhaul Falls – A tube slide that spirals through a waterfall and cave.

Hideaway Bay

Crush n' Gusher – Guests must be 48" (1.22m) or taller to ride. A roller coaster-style water slide with one to three person rafts – you go both downhill and uphill with the help of high-pressure jets. This is great fun and there are three different slides to choose from.

Miss Fortune Falls – Board this exciting family-raft attraction to spy the precious treasure artifacts collected by Captain Mary Oceaneer.

Typhoon Lagoon

Typhoon Lagoon Surf Pool – This star park attraction is the world's biggest outdoor wave pool. It alternates between 6-foot-high surfing waves every 90 seconds for 90 minutes, followed by small bobbing waves for 30 minutes. Waves are always small by the time they reach the shore.

A chalkboard at the edge of the beach posts the day's wave schedule. Inner tubes are not permitted in the lagoon.

Bay Slides – Slides for toddlers. Guests must be 60 inches or shorter to ride.

Creeks

Castaway Creek - A 2,100-foot lazy river that weaves through lush scenery around the whole park. Inner tubes are provided and a round trip takes 20 to 30 minutes.
Ketchakiddee Creek - A play area for younger kids with waterspouts and a small sandy beach. Guests must be 48" or *shorter* to ride the small slides in this area.

Dining
Happy Landings Ice Cream - Snacks, No DDP, desserts are $4.50-$14
Leaning Palms - Snacks and Quick Service, DDP accepted, entrées are $7.50-$13
Let's Go Slurpin' - Bar, No DDP, drinks are $6-$13
Lowtide Lou's - Snacks and Quick Service, DDP, accepted entrées are $10-$11
Snack Shack - Snacks, No DDP, snacks are $9.50-$11.50
Typhoon Tilly's - Snacks and Quick Service, Snacks, DDP accepted, entrées are $9.50-$11

Disney Springs

An exciting metropolis of restaurants, theaters and shops.

Disney Springs borders the south shore of Village Lake in the east-central portion of Walt Disney World. Self-parking at Disney Springs is free. Valet parking is $20.

Disney runs buses to and from Disney Springs from all Disney resort hotels. There are buses from the theme parks to Disney Springs from 4:00pm - but not from Disney Springs to the theme parks to avoid guests parking here for free and heading to the theme parks. To go from Disney Springs to

a theme park you must go to a hotel first.

There is boat transportation around Disney Springs, but the whole area is very walkable.

Bars and restaurants have varied opening and closing times but are usually open between 10:30am and 11:30pm (some locations open as early as 8:30am for breakfast).

Shops are generally open from 10:00am to 11:00pm

Monday through Friday, and 10:00am to 11:30pm on weekends. Some locations are open later.

Entertainment

Amphicars – Enjoy a guided tour on an amphicar on land and water. Pricing is $125 for up to 3 people with plus a captain. Available from 10:00am to 10:00pm daily.
Bibbidi Bobbidi Boutique – A magical salon to transform your children into little princesses and princes. Prices range from $20 to $450, plus tax. For ages 3 and up.
Disney's Photopass Studio – Add professional-style photoshoots to your PhotoPass account at no extra cost.
Marketplace Carousel – A small carousel.
Paradiso 37 Entertainment – Live evening entertainment.
Raglan Road Live Music – Live Irish-inspired music outside the venue.

Cirque Du Soleil - Drawn to Life

Disney describes the new show, opening in 2020: "This new show follows the story of Julie, a courageous and determined girl who discovers an unexpected gift left by her late father: an unfinished animation piece. Guided by a surprising pencil, she embarks on an inspiring quest sprinkled with her Disney childhood memories. Through this journey, she learns to imagine new possibilities and animate the story of her future."

AMC Movies

24 movie screens, with stadium-style seating in 18 theaters for unobstructed viewing. Includes six 'Fork & Screen' dine-in theaters.

House of Blues

Live music every night including blues, jazz, country and rock. Also home to the famous Gospel Brunch on Sundays.

Splitsville

A vintage, retro-style bowling alley with a fresh spin on music, dining and entertainment.

Aerophile - Balloon Flight

An iconic tethered balloon that sends guests soaring 400 feet into the sky, offering breath-taking views of the Walt Disney World Resort.

THE VOID: Step Beyond Reality

By combining state-of-the-art virtual-reality technology, physical stages and multi-sensory effects—including touch and smell—The VOID invites you to become active participants in uniquely themed environments.

Surrounded by 3D imagery and sound in an immersive story, you'll walk around freely without a tether as you explore an exciting new world.

At the time of writing both Star Wars and Wreck-It Ralph experiences are on offer. Pricing starts at $40 per person. Guests must be 48" (122 cm) or taller and at least 10 years old to visit The VOID.

NBA Experience

The NBA Experience is the ultimate place for basketball fans. You can dribble, shoot and dunk as you practice your skills, play interactive trivia games about the sport, head inside the player locker rooms and on the Draft Day stage, and much more. Tickets are $34 plus tax each.

Dining

All the dining locations below accept the Disney Dining Plan unless stated.

Drinks Lounges
• **Dockside Margaritas** – No DDP, drinks are $7.50-$17
• **Jock Lindsey's Hangar Bar** – No DDP, appetizers are $10-$12. Cocktails are up to $19.
• **Rainforest Café Lava Lounge** – appetizers are $11-$21, cocktails from $11.
• **Stargazers Bar** – No DDP, appetizers are $7-$11, drinks are $7-$110.

Quick Service
• **Blaze Fast-Fire'd Pizza** – Delicious pizzas ready in 180 seconds, pizzas are $8-$10.
• **Cookes of Dublin** – Irish food, entrées are $12-$15.
• **D-Luxe Burger** – American food, burgers are $10-$14.
• **Earl of Sandwich** – Sandwiches, salads and wraps are $6-$8.50.
• **Food Truck Park** – Disney Food Trucks selling food inspired by the parks. Each dish is $6 to $13.
• **Morimoto Asia Street Food** – Pan-Asian, entrées: $6-$14.
• **Pepe by José Andrés** – Spanish sandwiches, $8-$14.
• **Pizza Ponte** – Pizzas are $7-$8 for a slice or $9-$10 for a sandwich.
• **The Polite Pig** – American BBQ flavors, entrées: $12-$22.
• **The Smokehouse at House of Blues** – American food, entrées are $6-$14.
• **Wolfgang Puck Express** – entrées are $9-$20. Breakfast options: $8-$14.

Table Service
• **AMC Disney Springs 24 Dine-In Theatres** – No DDP, entrées are $11-$18.
• **The Boathouse** – American style, entrées are $13-$50. An upscale, waterfront dining experience with artwork and boats.
• **Chef Art Smith's Homecomin'** – Southern favorites from a glass-walled show kitchen and the Southern Shine Bar. Entrées are $18 to $30. At brunch, entrées are $17-$28.
• **City Works Eatery & Pour House** – Live sports bar. Brunch entrees are $15-$22.

Lunch and dinner entrées are $17 to $29.
• **The Edison** – Themed to a 1920s-period power plant. American food, craft cocktails and live entertainment. Entrées are $18-$24 at lunch and $20-$38 at dinner. Guests must be aged 21+ to enter The Edison after 10:00 p.m.
• **Enzo's Hideway** – Italian. Entrées: $24-$43. Sunday evenings, a family-style feast is $45 per adult and $19 per child.
• **Frontera Cocina** – American and Mexican food, entrées are $19-$38.
• **House of Blues** – American food, entrées are $16-$42.
• **Jaleo by José Andrés** – Spanish tapas cuisine. Entrees are $10 to $37.
• **Maria & Enzo's** – Italian cuisine, entrées are $17-$46 at brunch, $24-$46 at lunch and dinner.
• **Morimoto Asia** – Pan-Asian, Signature Dining, entrées are $19-$32. There is a lighter 'late night' menu with entrées at $13-$17.

- **Paddlefish** – Seafood, entrées are $17-$65.
- **Paradiso 37** – Entrées are $17-$38.
- **Planet Hollywood** – American food, entrées are $16-$30.
- **Rainforest Café** – American food, entrées are $17-$37.
- **Raglan Road Irish Pub and Restaurant** – Irish food, entrées are $12-$24 at lunch, $14-$29 at dinner, $14-$22 at brunch.
- **Splitsville Dining Room** – American food, entrées are $12-$26.
- **STK Orlando** – Rooftop Steakhouse, No DDP. Entrées are $11-$75 at lunch, $21-$253 at dinner, and $11-$74 at brunch.
- **T-REX** – American food, entrées are $18-$30.
- **Terralina Crafted Italian** – No DDP, entrées: $14-$44.
- **Wolfgang Puck Bar & Grill** – Mediterranean dishes.

Entrees are $17-$24.
- **Wine Bar George** – No DDP, entrées are $13-$72, drinks are $9-$60.

Speciality Food and Snacks
- **Amorette's Patisserie** – No DDP, pastries, cakes and crepes are $7 to $75.
- **AristoCrêpes** – Crepes:$7-$9
- **B.B. Wolf's Sausage Co.** – Sausage snacks: $9.50-$14
- **The Daily Poutine** – Canadian food, poutine: $10.
- **Disney's Candy Cauldron** – Candy and chocolates.
- **Erin McKenna's Bakery NYC** – Snacks are $2-$10.50.
- **The Ganachery** – A chocolate lover's dream.
- **Ghirardelli Soda Fountain** – Desserts are $6-$13, drinks are $5-$9.
- **Goofy's Candy Co.** – Candy, cookies, chocolates, frozen drinks and more.
- **Joffrey's Coffee & Tea Co.**

– Drinks are $3.50-$6. Alcoholic drinks are $12.
- **Sprinkles** – Cupcakes, No DDP, cupcakes: $5-$6, cookies: $3.50. There is even a Cupcake ATM.
- **Starbucks** – Drinks $3-$6.
- **Vivoli il Gelato** – Gelatos are $5.50-$7.50 and milkshakes are $10-$12.50. Serves Panini sandwiches, espresso drinks and gelato.
- **Wetzel's Pretzels** – Pretzels are $6-$10.
- **YeSake** – Snacks are $5.50-$10.

Shops

Fashion and Sportswear
Stores include American Threads, Anthropologie, Columbia, DisneyStyle, Everything But Water, Fit2Run, francesca's, Free People, JOHNNY WAS, kate spade new york, LACOSTE, Levi's, Lilly Pulitzer, Lucky Brand, lululemon, NBA Store, Pelé Soccer, Shore, Stance, Superdry, Tommy Bahama, Tren-D, Under Armour, UNIQLO, Volcom and ZARA.

Toys and Games
Stores include Dino-Store, The LEGO Store, Once Upon A Toy, and Star Wars Galactic Outpost, Star Wars Trading Post and Super Hero Headquarters.

Jewelry and Accessories
Stores include ALEX AND ANI, Chapel Hats, Coach, Edward Beiner, Erwin Pearl, Kipling, Luxury of Time, Na Hoku, Oakley, PANDORA, Something Silver, Sunglass Icon, TUMI, UNOde50 and Vera Bradley.

Footwear
Stores include Havaianas, Johnston & Murphy, Melissa Shoes, Sanuk, Sperry and UGG.

Home, Decor, Gifts and Speciality
Stores include The Art Corner, The Art of Disney, The Boathouse BOATIQUE,

Coca-Cola Store, Crystal Art, Disney's Days of Christmas, Disney's Pin Traders, Disney's Wonderful World of Memories, House of Blues Gear Shop, Marketplace Co-Op, Mickey's Pantry, Orlando Harley-Davidson, Pop Gallery, Rainforest Café Retail Village, Ron Jon Surf Shop, Shop for Ireland, Sosa Family Cigars, The Store at Planet Hollywood, Sugarboo & Co. and World of Disney Store.

Beauty and Health
Stores include The Art of Shaving, Basin, Kiehl's, M·A·C Cosmetics, L'Occitane en Provence, Origins, Savannah Bee Company and Sephora.

Activities Outside the Parks

Walt Disney World offers much more than just theme parks and water parks.

ESPN Wide World of Sports

This 200-acre sports complex hosts both professional and amateur sports games. There are three baseball fields, six NBA-sized basketball courts, softball courts, tennis courts, a track and field center, and beach volleyball courts.

Access to most amateur events can be purchased at the Box Office. Adult tickets are $19.50 and children's tickets are $14.50. Park tickets with the 'Park Hopper Plus' option may be used for entry to some events.

Access to the venue is available via limited buses from the All-Star Resorts, Caribbean Beach Resort and Pop Century Resort. Free parking is also available.

Ticket info is available on 407-939-GAME or at disneyworldsports.com.

Miniature Golf

Mini golf course rounds at Walt Disney World are $14 for adults & $12 per child.

Fantasia Miniature Golf
There are two different courses – Fantasia Gardens and Fantasia Fairways, both themed to Fantasia.

Fantasia Gardens is perfect for those new to mini-golf and kids; expect water

effects, creative obstacles and great theming. Fantasia Fairways is for the more experienced mini-golfers.

To get to Fantasia Minigolf, take a bus to either the Boardwalk or Swan hotels, then it is a short walk.

Winter Summerland Miniature Golf
There is a winter-themed

course and a summer-themed course. At the winter course you make your way through the course towards the 'North Hole'; at the summer course, there is beach theming.

The two courses are next to Blizzard Beach water park. You can drive there or take one of the resort buses.

Golf

Walt Disney World Golf Courses:
• **Magnolia Golf Course** – The main hazard on this 18-hole course is water.
• **Lake Buena Vista Golf Course** – This 18-hole golf course has hosted the PGA Tour, the LPGA Tour and USGA events.
• **Palm Golf Course** – An 18-hole golf course.
• **Oak Trail Golf Course** – This 9-hole family-friendly golf course is a walking distance course with a par of 36. There are junior tees for the smaller family members.

Pricing:
• $35 to $75 per person for each of the 18-hole courses. The Oak Trail Golf Course is $19 per junior (under 18) and $35 for adults. Disney hotel guests pay less. 2-round and 3-round passes are available.
• Free transportation for Disney hotel guests.
• Professional club rentals are available - $40-$65 for Magnolia, Buena Vista and Palm – and $15 for Oak Trail (a partial set). Junior club rentals are free at Oak Trail.
• 45-minute personal golf lessons are $75 for adults and $50 for under 18s.
• Replay rates are available at a 50% discount.

Other information:
• Golf cart use is included in your greens fee. Players must use golf carts on the 3 championship courses.
• Golf attire is required at all the golf courses; denim jeans or casual shorts are not permitted.
• Reservations at Disney's Magnolia Golf Course are recommended but not necessary. Walk-up golfers will try to be accommodated.
• For more detailed information on golfing, and to book tee times contact Disney directly on 407-WDW-GOLF or visit www.golfwdw.com.

Free Activities Outside the Parks

1. Visit the resort hotels

If you love the theming in the parks, visit the hotels. From the relaxing beach at the Polynesian Village Resort to the forest of the Wilderness Lodge, there is something for everyone.

Combine your trip to a resort with a meal. You do not need to be staying at the resorts to visit them. It is possible to spend three or four days simply visiting and exploring the dozens of Disney hotels. A must-do!

2. Movies under the stars

The Disney resort hotels offer nightly screenings of a Disney movie under the stars on a big screen. Chill out on one of the sun loungers sipping a cocktail while watching Toy Story or Fantasia.

3. Visit Disney's Boardwalk

This is a fun seaside-themed resort boardwalk area. You can often enjoy live entertainment such as jugglers, or you can explore the Boardwalk Resort and grab a bite to eat in one of the many restaurants.

4. Enjoy the Transportation

The monorail, ferryboat and The Skyliner all provide great views of the resort.

The hidden gems, however, are the boats between certain resorts and theme parks, such as the boat from the Wilderness Lodge to Fort Wilderness. This is a great, quaint, relaxing trip where all you see around you are trees and the lake.

Boats from Port Orleans, Old Key West and Saratoga Springs to Disney Springs also offer relaxing moments.

5. Sing around a camp-fire

Every evening, you can join Chip n' Dale in a sing-along around a camp-fire at Fort Wilderness Resort. There are optional marshmallows to buy to roast on the fire. After the camp-fire, there is a movie under the stars.

6. Watch a free parade

Every evening, the nighttime Electrical Water Pageant sails on the Seven Seas Lagoon. It is a simple flotilla, but it is worth seeing.

AllEars.net provides the following info on the timing:
• Polynesian Village Resort: 9:00pm
• Grand Floridian: 9:15pm
• Wilderness Lodge: 9:35pm
• Fort Wilderness: 9:45pm
• Contemporary Resort: 10:05pm
• Magic Kingdom Park: 10:20pm (during extended park hours).

When Magic Kingdom's fireworks are at 9:00pm, the Electrical Water Pageant runs 7 to 20 minutes later.

7. Fireworks from Polynesian Village Resort

Nothing can match standing in front of Cinderella Castle and seeing the nightly fireworks explode up close but for a different view, go to beach at the Polynesian Village Resort.

You can't see the projections from this distance but they do play the show music out of speakers at the Polynesian Village Resort walkway by the beach when the show begins. Arrive 45 minutes before the show.

8. Do a free Walt Disney World Resort hotel tour

Disney runs free tours of certain resort hotels. You do not need to be staying at the resorts to take these tours nor need reservations.

The 20-minute Sanaa Cultural Tour explores the Sanaa restaurant. It runs at 4:00pm daily. This tour may end with a tasty treat too! Call (407) 938-3000 to confirm this tour's schedule.

The Wonders of the Wilderness Lodge Tour is a 1-hour tour on the backstory and design of the Wilderness Lodge Resort. The tour runs Wednesdays to Saturdays at 9:00am. Call (407) 824-3200 to confirm this tour's schedule.

The Culinary Tour at Animal Kingdom Lodge is a food tour of the Boma and Jiko restaurants of about 30 minutes. You get to sample some of the food. Call (407) 938-3000 to confirm this tour's schedule.

Meeting the Characters

For many guests, a Walt Disney World vacation is not complete without meeting the characters in the parks.

In total, about 60 different characters meet in the parks daily. Some characters are 'random' appearances that are not published on the park schedule, others are 'scheduled' meets where you queue and take a photo, others are elaborate indoor experiences, and others like *Enchanted Tales with Belle* are more like interactive shows. You can also meet characters at select dining experiences.

If you need help finding a character, ask a Cast Member. Or, simply call 407-WDW-INFO.

Here we list character appearances that happen regularly and usually daily - these may change.

Magic Kingdom Park

- **Aladdin and Princess Jasmine** – Near *Aladdin's Magic Carpets* in Adventureland.
- **Alice in Wonderland** – By *Mad Tea Party* in Fantasyland
- **Ariel** – In *Ariel's Grotto* in Fantasyland.
- **Belle** – For those who take part in the show, you can take a photo with Belle at *Enchanted Tales with Belle.*
- **Buzz Lightyear** – Next to *Buzz Lightyear's Space Ranger Spin*.
- **Cinderella** – In *Princess Fairytale Hall* in Fantasyland.
- **Daisy and Donald Duck** – At *Pete's Silly Sideshow* in Fantasyland.

- **Elena of Avalor** – In *Princess Fairytale Hall*.
- **Gaston** – Outside *Gaston's Tavern* in Fantasyland.
- **Goofy** – At *Pete's Silly Sideshow* in Fantasyland.
- **Mary Poppins** – In Liberty Square Gazebo.
- **Merida** – In *Fairytale Garden*
- **Mickey Mouse** – *Town Square Theater*.
- **Minnie Mouse** – At *Pete's Silly Sideshow*.
- **Pluto** – At *Pete's Silly Sideshow*.
- **Peter Pan and Wendy** – Near *Peter Pan's Flight*.
- **Rapunzel** – All day in *Princess Fairytale Hall*.
- **Stitch** - In *Tomorrowland*
- **Tiana** – At *Princess*

Fairytale Hall.
- **Tinker Bell** (and fairy friends) – At *Town Square Theater*.
- **Winnie the Pooh and Tigger** – Near *The Many Adventures of Winnie the Pooh*.

Epcot

- **Aladdin and Princess Jasmine** – Morocco Pavilion
- **Anna and Elsa** – Norway Pavilion
- **Alice (in Wonderland)** – UK Pavilion
- **Aurora** - France Pavilion
- **Belle** – France Pavilion
- **Daisy Duck** – Near Spaceship Earth
- **Donald Duck** – Mexico Pavilion
- **Goofy** – Near the park entrance.
- **Joy (From 'Inside Out')** – in the Imagination pavilion.
- **Mary Poppins** – UK Pavilion
- **Mickey Mouse** – In the waiting area of *Disney-Pixar Short Film Festival*
- **Minnie Mouse** – World Showcase Gazebo
- **Mulan** – China Pavilion
- **Pluto** – Near the park entrance.
- **Snow White** – Germany Pavilion
- **Winnie the Pooh** – UK Pavilion
- **Wreck-it Ralph and Venellope** – in the Imagination pavilion.

Disney's Hollywood Studios

- **Buzz Lightyear, Woody & Green Army Men** – Near *Toy Story Midway Mania*
- **Cars Characters** – In *Cars Courtyard*
- **Chip & Dale** – Near Crossroads of the World.
- **Doc McStuffins** and **Fancy Nancy** – Outside *Disney Jr.*
- **Edna Mode** – At An Incredible Celebration.
- **Mickey (in his Sorcerer costume)** and **Minnie** – At *Red Carpet Dreams.*
- **Olaf** – At *Celebrity Spotlight*, by Echo Lake.
- **Pluto** – In Animation Courtyard.
- **Star Wars Characters** – At *Star Wars Launch Bay.*
- **Sulley** – At *Walt Disney Presents.*
- **The Incredibles** – In *Pixar Place.*

Disney's Animal Kingdom

- **Chip and Dale** – In Dinoland USA.
- **Donald and Daisy**– In Dinoland USA.
- **Dug and Russell** (from Up) – Near the entrance to *It's Tough to be a Bug.*
- **Goofy** – In Dinoland USA.
- **Mickey and Minnie** – At *Adventurers Outpost.*
- **Pocahontas** – At *Discovery Island Trails*
- **Pluto** – In Dinoland USA.
- **Rafiki** and **Timon** – At Rafiki's Planet Watch.
- **Scrooge McDuck** – In Dinoland USA.

Character Dining

Combine dining with meeting the characters at character-dining experiences.
- **Alice in Wonderland** – 1900 Park Fare, Grand Floridian (Breakfast only);
- **Beast** – Be Our Guest Restaurant (dinner only, Magic Kingdom)
- **Chip n Dale** – Garden Grill (Epcot)
- **Cinderella (and maybe Prince Charming)** – 1900 Park Fare, Grand Floridian (Dinner only); Cinderella's Royal Table (Magic Kingdom); Akershus Royal Banquet Hall (Norway pavilion, Epcot)
- **Donald Duck** – Tusker House in Disney's Animal Kingdom (and other ducks – Breakfast and Lunch); Cape May Café at Beach Club (Breakfast only); Chef Mickey's at Contemporary Resort (Brunch and Dinner)
- **Disney Junior Characters** (Sofia the First and Doc McStuffins) – Hollywood and Vine (Breakfast and Lunch, Disney's Hollywood Studios)
- **Lady Tremaine, Anastasia and Drizella** – 1900 Park Fare, Grand Floridian (Dinner)
- **Lilo and Stitch** – Ohana's Best Friends Breakfast, Polynesian Village Resort.
- **Goofy** – Cape May Café at Beach Club (Breakfast only); Chef Mickey's at Contemporary Resort (Brunch and Dinner); Tusker House at Animal Kingdom
- **Mad Hatter** – 1900 Park Fare, Grand Floridian (Breakfast only);
- **Mary Poppins** – 1900 Park Fare, Grand Floridian (Breakfast only), Princess Storybook Meals (Norway pavilion, Epcot)
- **Mickey Mouse** – Garden Grill (Epcot); Chef Mickey's at Contemporary Resort (Brunch and Dinner); Mickey's Backyard BBQ (Dinner only, Fort Wilderness Resort); Ohana's Best Friends Breakfast, Polynesian Village Resort;
- **Minnie Mouse** – Cape May Café, Beach Club (Breakfast only); Chef Mickey's at Contemporary Resort (Brunch and Dinner)
- **Pluto** – Garden Grill (Epcot); Chef Mickey's at Contemporary Resort (Brunch and Dinner); Ohana's Best Friends Breakfast, Polynesian Village Resort.
- **The Princesses** – Cinderella's Royal Table (Magic Kingdom); Akershus Royal Banquet Hall (Norway Pavilion, Epcot)
- **Winnie the Pooh, Tigger, Piglet and Eeyore** – Crystal Palace (Magic Kingdom), 1900 Park Fare, Grand Floridian (Breakfast only).

None of these character appearances are guaranteed but they are a good indication of who you can expect to see and where.

Doing Disney on a Budget

Visiting Walt Disney World is not exactly cheap, but it can be done on a budget, and you can still have a fantastic trip while saving some cash.

Planning

1. Staying On-Site – Do you need a Disney hotel? They are convenient but are often more expensive than off-site hotels. Remember to factor in costs like resort fees, taxes, parking and transportation when comparing.

2. Buy an annual pass – If you plan on visiting more than once in the same year, buying an annual pass can be a great money saver. If staying off-site, you will not need to pay for parking at the parks with an annual pass. It can also save you a lot of money on hotels, dining and merchandise.

3. Wait for a special offer – Walt Disney World often runs special offers – whether it is discounted room prices or free dining, so keep an eye out for these. Free dining offers, in particular, can save you a lot of money.

4. Downgrade your hotel – Do you need a luxury Disney hotel? Will you use the amenities you are paying for? If not, then downgrade to somewhere less expensive.

5. Tickets – Buy tickets online at reputable websites, e.g. undercovertourist.com – there are savings of up to $77 per person compared to buying from Disney. European visitors should consider the Ultimate Tickets, instead of buying tickets at American prices.

6. Quieter times – By visiting when the parks are less busy, you can do more each day and spend fewer days in the parks. See our quiet times section of this guide. Tickets are also cheaper during off-peak periods.

7. Don't bring a car – Disney hotel parking costs $15-$33 per night. Theme park parking is $25-$50 per day (theme park parking is free for Disney hotel guests).

At the Parks

1. Do not purchase a Dining Plan – Although the Dining Plans claim savings of up to 40%, if you don't eat a lot, or eat cheaper dishes, it's cheaper to pay for each meal individually.

2. Packed lunches – You can make your own meals, such as sandwiches, and take them into the parks. If you have a car, drive to a nearby supermarket for supplies.

3. Eat meals off-site – Drive off-property and eat outside of Walt Disney World. Food is often a fraction of the cost.

4. Table Service at lunch – Table Service meals and buffets are often cheaper at lunch than at dinner. The food on offer may be different or the same.

5. Take your own photos – Don't pay $15 or $20 for a character photo, simply take one yourself, ask another guest, or ask a Cast Member who will be happy to help.

6. Take your own merch – If your child will want to buy a dress or outfit in the parks, these are substantially cheaper online, at supermarkets or anywhere outside Walt Disney World. Buy them and pack them secretly. Give your child the costume once you arrive. The same applies to Disney plushes and toys.

7. More affordable meals – Some meals are better value than others. Kids' Quick Service meals, for example, are great value and include a drink, whereas adult meals do not.

Everything can be ordered a la carte - remove the fries if you don't them. Or, have a late lunch buffet and then a smaller snack for dinner.

Dining

There is a huge variety of places to eat at Walt Disney World, from sandwiches to fast food to Table Service dining, character buffets to signature options.

Restaurant Types

Buffet restaurants – Fill up your plate from the food offered as many times as you want. A variation is "family-style" meals where servers/waiters come around to tables and offer food.

Quick Service – Fast food. Everything from burgers and chips, to chicken to pizza and pasta, as well as more exotic options.

Table Service – Restaurants where you order from a menu, and are served by a waiter/server.

Character buffets – All-you-can-eat locations where characters visit each table to interact while you dine.

Signature Dining Experiences – The most exquisite dining experiences. These require two Table Service credits for guests on Disney Dining Plans.

Dinner Shows – A meal (usually buffet or family-style) is included in the price, as well as your entertainment for the evening. Dinner shows cost two Table Service credits for guests on Dining Plans.

Disney Dining Plans

Disney Dining Plans are pre-paid dining credits. Dining Plans are available to guests who book a vacation package with park tickets and a hotel, and Disney Vacation Club bookings.

Guest are allotted a number of 'credits' for each night of their stay for Table Service meals, Quick Service meals and Snacks. The number of credits depends on the plan purchased. Credits are redeemed for meals.

You are given all your credits as a lump sum at the beginning of your vacation; you choose how and when to use these by midnight on the night you check out.

Disney claims you can save up to 40% by purchasing the dining plans but this relies on you always eating the most expensive menu items.

You must book the Disney Dining Plans for the whole of your stay. You can get around this with two back-to-back hotel reservations, and only adding a Dining Plan to one.

Gratuities are not included with the dining plans except for Dinner Shows, Private In-Room Dining, and at Cinderella's Royal Table.

Merchandise or photo products that may be offered at some Character Dining Experiences are not included.

Reservations are strongly recommended for all Table Service restaurants - check menus at Disney.go.com/dining in advance to decide.

Top Tip: Present your MagicBand before ordering – restaurants often have two menus, with one specifically for those on Disney Dining Plans.

Top Tips

1: You do not have to order from the set menu, although it may save you money if you do. Ordering an item separately (a la carte) is completely fine.

2: Disney sometimes offers free dining to guests staying at its resort hotels that also book park tickets at the same time – if this offer is available, grab it with both hands as it can save you a significant amount of money.

3: Disney offers an allergy-friendly menu at almost all its Quick Service and Table Service restaurants. The allergy-friendly menus cover the most common allergies, including gluten, wheat, milk, peanut, nut and fish. If a guest wishes to speak to a chef, that option is available.

Mobile Ordering:
Many of the Quick Service restaurants allow you to order and pay using MyDisneyExperience without waiting in line. You will be notified when your food is ready. This saves you time during peak hours.

Here we list what is included per night of your stay with each Dining Plan for 2020. (Prices are per night and include tax)

Quick-Service Dining Plan	Dining Plan	Dining Plan Plus	Deluxe Dining Plan
$55 per adult, $26 per child (ages 3-9). • 2 Quick Service meals (entrée and non-alcoholic beverage) • 2 Snacks • 1 refillable resort mug per stay (worth $20)	$78.01 per adult, $30.51 per child. • 1 Quick Service meal • 1 Table Service meal (entrée and non-alcoholic beverage at breakfast OR entrée, dessert and non-alcoholic beverage at lunch and dinner. At buffets, you get access to the full buffet and a drink) • 2 Snacks • 1 refillable resort mug per stay (worth $20)	$94.60 per adult, $35 per child. • 2 Table Service or Quick Service meals. (For Table Service: entrée and non-alcoholic beverage at breakfast OR entrée, dessert and non-alcoholic beverage at lunch and dinner. At buffets, you get access to the full buffet and a drink) • 2 Snacks • 1 refillable resort mug per stay (worth $20)	$119 per adult, $47.50 per child. • 3 Table Service or Quick Service meals. You can choose for maximum flexibility. You also get an appetizer at Table Service locations, in addition to an entrée, dessert and non-alcoholic beverage. • 2 Snacks • 1 refillable resort mug per stay (worth $20)

At the end of your meal when you ask for the check, you will receive a receipt stating how many credits you used for that meal and how many remain. If you have bought several Dining Plans together, this number will be the sum of all your party's credits. You are free to order off-menu items and pay for these separately.

Reservations and Cancellations

At Table Service restaurants, we *strongly* recommend reservations. These can be made up to 180 days in advance at 407-WDW-DINE or online. At popular dining locations, such as *Cinderella's Royal Table*, you need to make reservations exactly 180 days in advance to dine at peak times.

A credit/debit card is required for dining reservations. Cancellations should be made the day before by 11:59pm; a $10 per person charge applies to no-shows.

Guests can also make last-minute dining reservations up to 20 minutes in advance using MyDisneyExperience.

Dress Codes

The following have a business casual dress code:
• Artist Point at Disney's Wilderness Lodge
• California Grill at the Contemporary Resort
• Cítricos at the Grand Floridian Resort & Spa
• Flying Fish Cafe at Disney's BoardWalk
• Jiko – The Cooking Place at Animal Kingdom Lodge
• Monsieur Paul at Epcot
• Narcoossee's at Disney's Grand Floridian Resort & Spa
• Takumi-Tei at Epcot
• Yachtsman Steakhouse at Yacht and Beach Club Resorts

Men's Dress Code: Dress slacks, jeans, pants, or dress shorts, short- or long-sleeved shirt with a collar or a t-shirt is required. Jackets are optional.

Ladies Dress Code: Jeans, skirt, or dress shorts with a blouse, sweater or t-shirt, or a dress required.

Not permitted: Tank tops, swimsuits or cover-ups, hats for men, cut offs, torn clothing, or t-shirts with offensive words or graphics.

Victoria and Albert's has a much stricter dress code - enquire when reserving.

Park Services

Many things can make or break a Walt Disney World vacation. This chapter covers important things to consider such as when to visit, and park services.

Photopass and Memory Maker

In the theme parks, you will find photographers ready to take your photo at major landmarks, at character meets and other locations.

Photopass:
Photopass works with a special card which you are given, at no cost, the first time you have a photo taken. You then use this same card every time you take photos, handing it to the photographer to scan. Once your trip is over, enter the code on your Photopass card into the Photopass website to see all your photos. From there, you can add your photos to souvenirs, order individual prints or pay for photo downloads.

Memory Maker:
Memory Maker is a photo package that allows you to purchase all your Photopass photos at once. This includes in-park photos, character photos, dining photos and on-ride photos.

Photos are available from the day they were taken until 45 days later. You have 30 days from the date of your first download to take more pictures with your

Memory Maker account.

It is available in advance for $169 or at Walt Disney World for $199. If you have a MagicBand, tap it each time to get your photos in the park. You can also buy a physical CD archive with all your pictures for an extra $30, or download the photos for free.

Guests who wear a MagicBand on rides have their attraction photos automatically added to their MyDisneyExperience account without needing to stop at the ride photo counter. The ride photo at *Frozen Ever After* is exclusive to MagicBand wearers.

In addition, riders with MagicBands on *The Twilight Zone: Tower of Terror* and *Seven Dwarfs Mine Train* have an on-ride video added to their account.

Although on-ride photos are usually linked automatically, it is still worth adding them manually as there can be errors. To do this, when you see the photo screens, tap your MagicBand on the reader below your photo.

A one-day Memory Maker package is available for $69. Guests can purchase the 'Memory Maker One Day' via the My Disney Experience app after having linked one photo.

Top Tip 1: Pre-purchase MemoryMaker in advance at disneyworld.Disney.go.com/memory-maker/ to save $30. This must be done at least 3 days before your first photo is taken.

Top Tip 2: Take a photo of your Photopass card and its barcode, so if you lose the card you still have access to all the photos on it.

Top Tip 3: You can have multiple Photopass cards and add them all to one online account in one go.

On-Ride Photos

Many rides have specially placed cameras positioned to take perfectly framed photos of you on the ride. After the ride, you can purchase these photos and save the memory.

You do not have to buy on-ride photos straight after your ride; you can pick them up at any time during the day - remember your number at the ride exit. If you like the photo - buy it!

Single Rider Queue Lines

One of the best ways to significantly reduce your time waiting in queue lines is to use the Single Rider line instead of the regular standby queue line. This is a completely separate queue line that is used to fill free spaces on ride vehicles - guests who join this line will ride individually.

As an example of how the system works: if a ride vehicle can seat 8 people and a group of 4 turns up,

followed by a group of 3 in the regular standby line, then a guest from the Single Rider line will fill the empty space.

If the park gets extremely busy then Single Rider lines can be closed when the wait for Single Riders is the same or greater than the regular line, undermining its purpose. If the park is not very busy then sometimes these queue lines do not operate either.

Groups can use the Single Rider queue line; they will not ride with each other but can still meet after riding at the exit of the ride.

The following rides have single rider queue lines:
• *Expedition Everest* (Animal Kingdom)
• *Rock n Roller Coaster* (Hollywood Studios)
• *Test Track (*Epcot)
• *Millennium Falcon: Smugglers Run* (Hollywood Studios)

Extra Magic Hours

Each day, Disney resort hotel guests are allowed 1-hour early entry into one theme park, or can stay up to 2 hours after regular park closing at another park.

During these extended opening hours, wait times for rides are typically much shorter than during the day. Each member of your party needs a valid resort ID to access attractions during these extended hours.

The exact parks open during Extra Magic Hours (EMH) vary week to week and can be seen online up to 6

months in advance on the Walt Disney World website.

How can I get Extra Magic Hours?
They are available exclusively to guests staying at Walt Disney World resort hotels and select partner properties. Annual pass holders not staying at Disney hotels are not entitled to EMH.

What rides are available during EMH?
Unfortunately, not all rides are open during these extended hours, but most popular rides (not shows)

are open - Disney does not publish an exact list.

As of May 2020, *Star Wars: Rise of the Resistance* is not available during Extra Magic Hours.

Rider Switch

Rider Switch is a system that enables a group to take turns riding an attraction while only needing to wait once. An example use is when a child is too small and adults take turns riding so the other can stay with the child.

To use Rider Switch, simply ask a Cast Member at an attraction entrance to use

the service.

Group 1 (for example, the father) will go through the normal queue line and Group 2 (for example, the mother) will be given a return time as a digital Rider Switch Pass on their park tickets or MagicBands. The return time will start roughly when Group 1 has returned and last for

1h10m.

Once Group 1 has ridden, Group 2 passes the child to Group 1 and enters the ride through the FastPass+ entrance. Up to 3 people may ride with this pass.

Rider Switch is available at all attractions with a minimum height limit.

When to Visit

Crowds vary significantly from season to season and even day to day. The difference in a single day can save you hundreds of dollars and hours of waiting. You need to consider public holidays and school vacations in the U.S.A. and surrounding countries, the weather, pricing and more to find the best time to go.

Major Holidays in 2020:
• 1st to 5th January: New Year's Day & School Break
• 17th to 21st January: Martin Luther King Jr. Day and Weekend

• 13th to 25th February: Presidents Day & School Break
• 1st March to 19th April: Spring Break and Easter
• 22nd to 26th May: Memorial Day Weekend
• Mid-June to Mid-August: Summer School Break (particularly busy around 4th July)
• 5th to 8th September: Labor Day Weekend
• 9th to 13th October: Columbus Day Weekend
• 7th to 16th November: Veterans Day Week
• 20th to 30th November: Thanksgiving Week

• 18th December to 4th January: Christmas and New Year's

Best times to visit in 2020:
• Early to mid-January
• Between Presidents Day and Spring Break
• Mid-April to mid-May (avoiding Easter and Spring Break)
• Late-May to Mid-June
• Mid-August to early-October (avoiding Labor Day Weekend)
• End of November to mid-December

Park Regulations

Here are some notable park regulations which you should be aware of:
• Proper attire, including shoes and shirts, must be worn. Anyone wearing inappropriate attire may be removed from the park.
• Smoking (including vaping) is not allowed in the parks.
• Guests under age 14 must be accompanied by another guest aged 14 or older to enter the theme parks and water parks.

• Recreational devices with wheels such as skateboards, scooters, skates or shoes with built-in wheels are not permitted.
• Strollers larger than 31" x 52" are not permitted.
• Any item of baggage or a cooler larger than 24" x 15" 18" is not permitted in the parks.
• Trailer-like items pushed or towed by a person or a machine are not permitted.
• Weapons, masks, folding

chairs, large tripods, glass containers, alcoholic beverages, illegal substances, and animals that are not service animals are not permitted.
• Balloons, plastic straws and drink lids are not permitted at *Disney's Animal Kingdom Park* for the safety of the animals.
• Selfie sticks are banned from all Disney theme parks and water parks.

Stroller Rentals

Strollers, also known as buggies or pushchairs, can be rented at the entrance to the four theme parks.

A single stroller, for children of 50lbs of less, is $15 per day, or $13 as part of a

multi-day purchase.

A double stroller for children of 100lbs or less is $31 per day, or $27 as part of a multi-day purchase.

Strollers must be returned

on the same day and cannot leave the theme parks.

You can use the same receipt to hire strollers at all four theme parks on the same day. Strollers can also be rented at Disney Springs.

"Play Disney Parks" App

At some point you will find yourself in a queue line wondering how to pass the time - Disney has the answer with the free 'Play Disney Parks' app. This includes ride-specific games and trivia, music, and other cool interactive features. Plus, the app can let you interact with things outside the queue lines - such as many of the elements in *Star Wars: Galaxy's Edge*.

Useful Phone Numbers

- **Main Street USA Barber Shop Appointments**: 407-824-6550
- **Central Lost and Found**: 407-824-4245
- **Central Reservations Office (CRO)**: 407-934-7639
- **Disney Dining Reservations**: 407-WDW-DINE
- **Main Disney Switchboard**: 407-824-2222
- **Firework Cruises**: 407-939-7529
- **Florist and Gift Basket Department**: 407-827-3505 (disneyflorist.com)
- **Golf**: 407-WDW-GOLF
- **Guest Services Mail Order**: 407-363-6200
- **Kennel**: 407-824-6568
- **Resort Medical Care**: 407-648-9234
- **Recreation**: 407-WDW-PLAY
- **Reservations**: 407-934-7639
- **Walt Disney World Transportation**: 407-824-4321
- **WDW Operation Information (Hours etc.)**: 407-WDW-INFO

To dial the USA from international locations, you will need to add '+1' before these phone numbers.

Height Restrictions

Although we cover height restrictions throughout the parks section of this travel guide, this section gives you an overview of all the height restrictions in one place.

Do not try to fraudulently increase the apparent height of your child through heels or other measures. Attractions Cast Members will ask for these to be removed before measuring. Height restrictions are in place for the safety of all guests. No exceptions are made.

- **Alien Swirling Saucers** – Disney's Hollywood Studios – 32" (0.81m)
- **Tomorrowland Speedway** – Magic Kingdom Park – 32" (0.81m) to ride with an adult, or 54" (1.37m) to drive alone.
- **Kali River Rapids** – Animal Kingdom Park – 38" (0.97m)
- **Slinky Dog Dash** – Disney's Hollywood Studios – 38" (0.97m)
- **Seven Dwarfs Mine Train** – Magic Kingdom Park – 38" (0.97m)
- **Millennium Falcon: Smugglers Run** – Disney's Hollywood Studios – 38" (0.97m)
- **Star Wars: Rise of the Resistance** – Disney's Hollywood Studios – 40" (1.02m)
- **Big Thunder Mountain Railroad** – Magic Kingdom Park – 40" (1.02m)
- **Splash Mountain** – Magic Kingdom Park – 40" (1.02m)
- **Dinosaur** – Animal Kingdom Park – 40" (1.02m)
- **Star Tours** – Disney's Hollywood Studios – 40" (1.02m)
- **The Twilight Zone: Tower of Terror** – Disney's Hollywood Studios – 40" (1.02m)
- **Soarin'** – EPCOT – 40" (1.02m)
- **Expedition Everest** – Animal Kingdom Park – 44" (1.12m)
- **Mission: SPACE** – EPCOT – 44" (1.12m)
- **Space Mountain** – Magic Kingdom Park – 44" (1.12m)
- **Avatar Flight of Passage** – Animal Kingdom Park – 44 inches (1.12m)
- **Primeval Whirl** – Animal Kingdom Park – 48" (1.22m)
- **Rock 'n' Roller Coaster** – Disney's Hollywood Studios – 48" (1.22m)

Additional height restrictions apply at the Disney water parks.

Spend Less Time in Lines

1. Disney hotel guests - At Disney hotels (and select other hotels), you get Extra Magic Hours (EMH) which give you one hours' early entry into one theme park each day, or you can stay up to two hours in another park in the evening. Most popular attractions are open.

Morning Extra Magic Hours are extremely valuable, as most people do not want to get up early, so you can hit many of the headline attractions in this first hour! Evening Extra Magic Hours are busier than the morning ones but ride waits are less than during regular hours.

2. Visit a non-EMH park – Disney's 30,000+ on-site hotel rooms mean the park with evening Extra Magic Hours is much busier than others. Go to a different park in the day, and visit the park with EMH only during the extended opening hours – you need a park hopper ticket. If you don't have EMHs, avoid parks on their EMHs day as they are busy with no extra benefit to you.

3. Use Character Breakfast entrances at park opening – Look for the park entrances marked "Character Breakfast". These are for guests eating in-park character breakfasts until park opening. From park opening, they are open to everyone!

4. See our 'When to Visit' section – If you are going on New Year's Day, expect to queue for a lot longer than in the middle of September.

5. The Parks Open Early – *Magic Kingdom Park* opens 1 hour before the scheduled opening time. You wait in front of *Cinderella Castle* until the opening show. You can explore Main Street, U.S.A. during this time.

Epcot frequently opens its gates 15 minutes or more before its official opening time. Some rides will be running straight away.

Disney's Hollywood Studios opens its gates 15 to 45 minutes before the official opening time. Some rides run straight away.

At *Disney's Animal Kingdom Park*, gates usually open 30 to 45 minutes before the official time. *Kilimanjaro Safaris, Expedition Everest* and *Avatar Flight of Passage* usually open soon after this.

6. Do the popular rides first – If you arrive at park opening, ride popular attractions in the first hour! Head to these first.
• Magic Kingdom Park: *Seven Dwarfs Mine Train, Peter Pan's Flight* and *Space Mountain.*
• Epcot: *Frozen Ever After, Ratatouille,* and *Test Track.*
• Disney's Hollywood Studios: *Slinky Dog Dash, Mickey and Minnie's Runaway Railway* and *Toy Story Midway Mania.*
• Disney's Animal Kingdom Park: *Avatar Flight of Passage, Na'vi River Journey*

and *Expedition Everest.*

7. Post-firework riding – Check when the nighttime show is performed. If the park remains open after, you can ride attractions until the park closes. At night, WAITS should be minimal. If you want a last-minute ride, get in the queue line before park closing to ride!

8. Ride outdoor rides during the rain – Outside rides such as *Dumbo, Slinky Dog Dash, Splash Mountain* and *Big Thunder Mountain* have much shorter waits when it is raining. You may get soaked, but your wait will be shorter! During thunder, outdoor attractions temporarily stop operation.

9. Go shopping at the start or end of the day – Even when the park is officially closed in the evening, shops on Main Street, U.S.A., and other major shops in other parks stay open until most guests have left. Or, do your shopping at Disney Springs! Better yet, visit your resort hotel's own Disney store.

10. Extra paid options - Disney offers early entry to certain attractions for an extra fee ($89 per adult/$79 per child) with its Early Morning Magic event on select dates. Breakfast is also included.

2020 Seasonal Events

From marathons to food tasting and floral exhibits, there is something always something unique happening at Walt Disney World

Walt Disney World Marathon Weekend
Jan 8-12, 2020
This annual event features a 26.2-mile race through all four Disney parks. There is also a half marathon, a 5km run and the Walt Disney World 10K.

Epcot International Festival of the Arts
Jan 17 - Feb 24, 2020
Explore the visual arts with galleries, workshops and seminars. Then try new food with the culinary arts. Finally, enjoy performing arts from acrobatics to living statues and Broadway talent.

Disney Princess Half Marathon Weekend
Feb 20-23, 2020
This predominantly women's Half Marathon allows guests to celebrate all the qualities of a princess. The event includes a two-day health and fitness expo geared towards women, a family fun run of 5K and kids' races, as well as a 10K.

Epcot International Flower & Garden Festival
Mar 4 - Jun 1, 2020
Future World and World Showcase bloom with more than 30 million colorful blossoms, garden activities for kids and workshops with national gardening experts.

Guests can taste delights from over a dozen food-and-beverage marketplaces surrounding the World Showcase Lagoon. Plus, there are free concerts.

Star Wars Rival Run Half Marathon Weekend
Apr 16-19, 2020
Runners can enjoy a Star Wars experience, including medals and merchandise. This event includes a 5K, 10K, kids races, and half marathon! Canceled due to COVID-19.

Mickey's Not-So-Scary Halloween Party
Select dates Aug to Oct 2020
A family-friendly fright-fest at Magic Kingdom. You can expect Halloween shows, Mickey's "Boo-to-You" Halloween Parade, Halloween-themed fireworks, modified rides, treat trails and much more.

This party is an extra charge: Tickets are $85-$149 per adult and $80-$144 per child, plus tax. Tickets often sell out in advance.

Epcot International Food & Wine Festival
Select dates Aug to Sep 2020
Festival highlights include 30 food and beverage marketplaces; dining experiences with world-renowned chefs; culinary demos and beverage seminars; concerts; over 270 chefs including culinary stars; and the *Party for the Senses* grand tasting events.

Most festival entertainment is included in regular park admission. There are over 200 food-and-beverage items with each tapas-sized portion or drink at $4-$10.

Disney Wine & Dine Half Marathon Weekend
Nov 5-8, 2020
The ultimate "Runners'

Night Out" features a half marathon. Then, celebrate the win at an exclusive after-hours' party. The weekend also includes kids' races, a 5K family run, and an expo.

Mickey's Very Merry Christmas Party
Select dates Nov to Dec 2020
This party allows guests to delight in some holiday cheer. During the party, guests can experience the castle sparkling with thousands of white lights; Mickey's Once Upon A Christmastime Parade featuring classic Disney characters, elves, toy soldiers and even Santa; a Holiday-themed music and fireworks show; several stage shows; a seasonal version of Monsters Inc. Laugh Floor and Space Mountain, a Christmas light switch-on; snowfall on Main Street, U.S.A. and much more! Guests also get complimentary hot cocoa and cookies all night long.

Adult prices are $105 to $155, and child tickets are at $100 to $150. Tax is extra.

Epcot, Hollywood Studios, Disney Springs and Animal Kingdom also all offer their own Holiday entertainment at no extra charge.

A Special Thanks

Thank you very much for reading our travel guide to Walt Disney World and Universal Orlando. We hope that we have made a big difference to your vacation and you have found some tips that will save you time and money! Remember to take this guide with you while you are on vacation and use it in the parks.

....

If you have any questions or feedback, please use the 'Contact Us' section on our website at www.independentguidebooks.com.

If you have enjoyed this guide, you will want to check out:
• The Independent Guide to Universal Studios Hollywood
• The Independent Guide to Disneyland
• The Independent Guide to Tokyo Disney Resort
• The Independent Guide to Shanghai Disneyland
• The Independent Guide to Hong Kong Disneyland
• The Independent Guide to Disneyland Paris
• The Independent Guide to Paris
• The Independent Guide to London
• The Independent Guide to New York City
• The Independent Guide to Hong Kong
• The Independent Guide to Tokyo
• The Independent Guide to Dubai

Have a magical day!

Photo Credits:
The following photos have been used under a Creative Commons 2.0 Attribution License.

Anna Fox for Test Track; Benjamin Esham for Illuminations; Darren Wittko for photos of Animal Kingdom Lodge, and Pirates of the Caribbean; Daryl Mitchell for Pop Century; Darryl Kenyon for Kali River Rapids; d.k.peterson (Flickr user) for Disney Princess Half Marathon; Mark & Paul Luukkonen for Princess Fairytale Hall, Canada Pavilion and The Barnstormer; 'Flickr mjurn' for Old Key West; Greg Goebel for Astro Orbiter; Harshlight (Flickr user) for photos of Mad Tea Party, Seven Dwarfs Mine Train and Peter Pan's Flight; Inzakira (Flickr user) for Living with the Land; Jeff Kays for Blizzard Beach, Buzz Lightyear Space Ranger Spin and Soarin; Joseph Brent for ESPN Wide World of Sports; Justin Ennis for Jungle Cruise; Kyosuke Takayama for Norway Pavilion; Leigh Caldwell for the Halloween Party photo; Lou Oms for Imagination Pavilion; Luis Brizzante for Holiday Wishes and Spaceship Earth; Matthew Freeman for Splash Mountain; Michael Gray for photos of Mickey's Philharmonic, Monster's Inc, Caribbean Beach resort, Epcot Food and Wine festival, and Holiday Splendor; Michelle Tribe for Coronado Springs; Paul Hudson for Disney Springs and Mexico Pavilion; 'Paula and Cathy' for Turtle Talk; Phil Whitehouse for Cinderella Castle, in Fantasyland Section of guide; QuesterMark (Flickr user) for Contemporary Resort; Rhys A for Beach Club; rickpilot_2000 (Flickr user) for Typhoon Lagoon and Dinosaur; Sam Howzit for The Many Adventures of Winnie the Pooh, Very Merry Christmas Party, Big Thunder Mountain and it's a small world; Sonja - Epcot Holidays around the World; Wikimedia for Primeval Whirl and Flower and Garden Festival; zannaland (Flickr user) for Sorcerer's of the Magic Kingdom and The Barnstormer; Big Front Page Image - Phillie Casablanca, Back Castle at night photo - Frank H Phillips; Sorcerers of the Magic Kingdom - zannaland; Tom Sawyer Island - Chad Sparkes; Philharmagic - Sam Howzit; Turtle Talk with Crush, Jedi Training, Triceratop Spin - Theme Park Tourist; Voyage of the Little Mermaid - Loren Javier; Walt Disney Presents, Epcot Festival of the Arts, Cinderella Castle (cover) - Harshlight; Indiana Jones - Thomas Jung; Gorilla - Corey Ann; "it all started with a mouse" - Disney Parks Blog; Up! A Great Bird Aventure - Joel (coconut wireless); Na'vi River Journey - mliu92; and Lego Store - mrice1996;

Universal Globe - Alison Sanfacon; Photos of all on-site hotels, Hollywood Rip Ride Rocket, Jimmy Fallon, Fast and Furious, Shrek 4-D, Cabana Bay Bus, Reign of Kong, Spider-Man ride and character photo, Nightlife/Rising Star, CityWalk Dining/Cowfish, Mini Golf, Universal Dining Plan, Antojitos, Quick Service photo, Tri-Wizard Tournament, Blue Man Group, Aventura Hotel, Cinematic Spectacular and Rock the Universe - Universal Orlando; Men in Black, Woody Woodpecker's Nuthouse Coaster, One Fish Two Fish, Storm Force Accelatron, Pteranodon Flyers and Single Rider - Jeremy Thompson; Animal Actors on Location, Planning/Staff and Express Pass, Character Meets with Sideshow Bob - Theme Park Tourist; Chad Sparks - Hogwarts Express; Diagon Alley - osseus; Q-Bot - accesso.com; Refillable Mug - Universal Orlando; Nintendo Logo - Nintendo Co., Ltd; Volcano Bay - Paulo Guereta; Diagon Alley - amyr_81; Height requirements - Theme Park Tourist; Aventura Hotel, new york city streets and Sapphire Falls- Rain0975; Despicable Me - simon17964; Gringotts - Chris Favero; Hagrid's Motorbike Adventure - Rain097;

HARRY POTTER, characters, names and related indicia are trademarks of © Warner Bros. Entertainment Inc. Harry Potter Publishing Rights and © JKR. Logos, characters and brands are trademarks of their respective owners.

Made in the USA
Monee, IL
22 August 2021